THE TOMB OF AGAMEMNON

CATHY GERE

HARVARD UNIVERSITY PRESS

Cambridge, Massachusetts

2006

First published in Great Britain in 2006 by

Profile Books Ltd
3A Exmouth House
Pine Street
Exmouth Market
London ECIR OJH

Library of Congress Cataloging-in-Publication Data
Gere, Cathy, 1964–
The tomb of Agamemnon / Cathy Gere.
p. cm. — (Wonders of the World)
Includes bibliographical references and index.
ISBN 0-674-02170-3 (alk. paper)
1. Mycenae (Extinct city) 2. Excavations (Archaeology)—Greece—Argolis.
3. Agamemnon (Greek mythology) 4. Argolis (Greece)—Antiquities.
I. Title. II. Wonders of the world (Cambridge, Mass.)
DF221.M9G47 2006   938'.8—dc22   2005054695

Printed in the United Kingdom
by Butler and Tanner

CONTENTS

INTRODUCTION:

NARNIA ON THE PELOPONNESE

A LEGEND WITH A HUMAN FACE

The Mask of Agamemnon is the *Mona Lisa* of prehistory. On a summer's day in Athens it is almost impossible to get a glimpse of it, so thick are the crowds that throng round its case in the central hall of the National Archaeological Museum. But when a gap finally appears in the swarm of tourists, it does not disappoint. Beaten from a sheet of gold more than 3000 years ago to fit the corpse of a king of Mycenae, the face portrayed is startlingly individual. This was a handsome man, with a long aquiline nose, high cheekbones and a thin, wide mouth. He boasts a finely shaped handlebar moustache and trim beard with a chic little tuft of hair under his lower lip. Even in death his expression seems stern, with perhaps a trace of his legendary temper perceptible in the compressed line where his lips meet. Here, it seems, is the portrait of an actual person (illustration 1).

Instantly recognisable, and always a good selling point, the mask graces not only the dust jacket of this book, but also adorns countless tourist brochures and websites. It appears on the label of an eye-watering Greek brandy and frowns from the front of the Penguin Classics edition of Aeschylus'

Oresteia trilogy. Hundreds of replicas are for sale in souvenir shops all over Greece, in the form of earrings, cufflinks, pendants and paperweights. Its canonical status is only confirmed by its popping up where it shouldn't, for example on the cover of a book about the Trojan treasure, a hoard of gold dug up several hundred kilometres from where the mask was found. Invariably presented full frontal, cut out, floating in the empty space of its singularity and its fame, the image of this one artefact stands in for all the mystery and excitement of Greek archaeology. The Mask of Agamemnon represents the human face of Homeric epic, a recognisable individual through whom mortal life seems to be breathed into immortal legend.

The hero whose face supposedly slept beneath those golden features must qualify as one of the most unpleasant and miserable characters in an ancient literature strewn with unfortunate protagonists. Born into great wealth and power as heir to the kingdom of Mycenae, Agamemnon also inherited a terrible ancestral curse, originating, in some versions of the story, with the grisly deeds of his great-grandfather Tantalus, who boiled his son and served him to the gods. His father, Atreus, following the family tradition, murdered his two little nephews and tricked his brother into eating their flesh. Agamemnon duly came into his patrimony, curse and all, and succeeded to the throne of the richest city in Greece. In accordance with his political pre-eminence, he was appointed commander-in-chief of the Greek forces for the Trojan War, whereupon the family curse really began to bite. Before the army had even set off, he was called upon to sacrifice the life of his daughter in order to procure favourable winds for the Greek ships. Having obediently dispatched

1. The so-called 'Mask of Agamemnon', one of the most instantly
recognizable archaeological artefacts of all time, here shown in its familiar
front view but also, more unusually, in profile.

her and been wafted to the Troad on the breath of divine appeasement, Agamemnon then became mired in a military stalemate. At the end of this decade-long stand-off he led his troops to the brink of disaster by squabbling with his best lieutenant over a couple of beautiful girls. Luckily for the Greeks, the two men made up just in time to achieve a costly victory over the Trojans, and Agamemnon returned to Mycenae with every reason to expect a hero's welcome. But no sooner had he reached home than he died abruptly and ingloriously, murdered by his wife Clytemnestra and her lover Aegisthus.

The origins of the myths of Agamemnon are lost in the gloom of the so-called Greek dark ages, when he was one of a large cast of heroes, demigods and gods in a mythology transmitted by the spoken word. In the eighth century BC, just as the darkness was giving way to the first glimmerings of literacy, the poet (or poets) known as Homer distilled the well-worn cycle of stories about the Trojan War into two epic poems, the closest thing to a bible ever possessed by pagan Greece. In the *Iliad* Agamemnon springs into life as a character full of tensions and contradictions, a king of kings with the flaws of an everyman. Although Homer commands the muse to sing of the anger of Achilles in the famous opening lines of the poem, it is actually Agamemnon whose unedifying combination of lust, arrogance and selfishness angers the gods in the first place and whose stubbornness splits the army into two factions. In the *Odyssey* Agamemnon's furious ghost appears to Odysseus to relate the story of his murder.

In the centuries that followed Agamemnon – courageous and powerful, but also cursed, quarrelsome, despotic and reckless – became a figure across whose life and death the greatest

Greek playwrights interrogated their moral, theological and political dilemmas. Starting with Aeschylus' famous cycle of plays on Agamemnon's murder and its consequences, the king of kings' irresistible combination of curse and character flaw supplied a rich vein of material for exploring the ethics of heroism, the relationship between fate and freedom, and the all-important difference between justice and vengeance. These writers, in full pursuit of the deeper truths to be found in fiction, did not scruple to change the Homeric stories, tailoring characters and situations to fit their own artistic and didactic purposes.

The challenge for Greek historians, on the other hand, was to establish how much actual historical reality could be credited to the Homeric epics – which events were, as James Joyce so elegantly put it, 'lodged in the room of the infinite possibilities they have ousted'. Although the historicity of the Trojan War itself was never questioned, the details of the narrative clearly owed more to the demands of poetry than of accuracy. Beginning with Herodotus' *Persian Wars*, various attempts were made to rationalise the epics, to come up with a plausible account of the causes of the Trojan War and to calculate its date using the genealogies preserved in the king-lists of Sparta. Herodotus himself dated the war to 800 years before his own time, i.e. approximately 1250 BC, and his guess is still just about as good as ours.

The same questions continued to vex and divide scholars for centuries. As Christianity took hold, Agamemnon began to shift over to the wrong side of the boundary between myth and history. St Augustine pronounced Homer deathly boring and one of his contemporaries declared that the Trojan War had never taken place. Although the pagan bard became wildly fashionable again when Christian orthodoxy loosened its grip in the eighteenth and nineteenth centuries, the veracity of the epics seemed more doubtful than ever. In 1846 the historian George Grote famously asserted that Greek history could only be said to start with the first Olympiad in 776 BC. Stories of earlier ages, he said, were nothing more than legends, empty of useful historical information, belonging to 'a region essentially mythical, neither approachable by the critic nor measurable by the chronographer'. He admitted that the Trojan War was of 'wider and larger interest' than other legends, but warned that it was 'a mistake to single it out from the rest as if it rested upon a different and more trustworthy basis'. It did not help that the city of Troy seemed to have disappeared, possibly buried under the later overbuilding of the small Hellenistic town of Ilium Novum or New Troy.

For those who clung to a belief in the historical truth of Homer, however, there was some comfort to be had in a remote corner of the north-eastern Peloponnese, where the walls of Agamemnon's Mycenae were still visible. These rudely grand remains seemed to bear mute witness to the reality of Homer's Age of Heroes. Their very existence raised a host of questions in the minds of the bard's believers. Was it through that great stone gate surmounted with sculpted lions that the lord of men, Agamemnon, had led his troops to war? Was the palace where he had met his untimely end somewhere on the acropolis? Above all, where was he buried? Did Clytemnestra and Aegisthus throw out his bones to be consumed by dogs and vultures? Or did his murderers bury Agamemnon with a show of honour and inter him in one of the splendid beehive-shaped buildings outside the walls or in a tomb somewhere within the citadel?

A mere quarter-century after George Grote dismissed the Trojan War as a fit subject only for poets and dreamers, the pendulum swung wildly back in the opposite direction. In 1872, the evangelical Homeric literalist Heinrich Schliemann burst on to the world stage brandishing a trowel, announcing that he had discovered and excavated the remains of Troy. A few years later, determined to locate the Tomb of Agamemnon, he began his assault on Mycenae. He mobilised a large workforce to clear the rubble and dirt of millennia from a promising spot inside the acropolis, and in the wet winter of 1876, deep below the surface of the ground, found five rock-cut tombs – 'shaft graves' – containing seventeen corpses covered in masses of gold jewellery. It appeared, Schliemann announced, that all seventeen had been slaughtered and buried at the same time. One of them – the mortal remains of an unusually tall man wearing a gold death mask – he identified as the very body of Agamemnon, the Homeric king of kings, murdered and buried along with his retinue (the other sixteen bodies) by his faithless wife and her paramour.

It is hard to overestimate the excitement generated by Schliemann's announcement that he had found Agamemnon's tomb. For the classically educated classes of the late nineteenth century, the *Iliad* and the *Odyssey* stood alongside the Christian Bible as the founding texts of Western civilisation, pagan scriptures that had enchanted many a Victorian childhood with the magic of their heroes, gods and impossibly beautiful women. By exhuming this legendary cast of characters and anchoring the gruesome story of Agamemnon's murder in material reality, it was as though Schliemann had brought these fairy tales to life – as though Narnia had been discovered on the Peloponnese. Even the sceptics had to admit that he was on to something. The gold he had found was dazzling: describing the precious objects from one tomb alone took up nearly fifty pages of his excavation report. In the wake of Schliemann's excavations, people began to beat a path to Mycenae. After stopping off in Athens to admire the gold hoard (which had been whisked off to the Greek capital shortly after its excavation), thousands of tourists came to look down into the deep shaft where Agamemnon's body had been found.

Seekers of any political stripe, it seemed, could find an ancestor, an inspiration or an enemy in the Mycenaean shaft graves. Friedrich Nietzsche applied his particular brand of proto-sociobiology to the newly 'real' Homeric heroes and came up with his ruthless aristocratic creed for a godless age. Sigmund Freud argued that Mycenaean civilisation existed not just as an archaeological layer in the history of Europe but also as a psychic stratum in the unconscious of every European. The Mycenaeans were celebrated by the Nazis as swastika-wielding Teutonic military geniuses. Greek nationalists recast Agamemnon's conflict with Troy as the forerunner of their own struggle with the Muslim Ottomans. Feminists lamented the patriarchal order introduced by the Mycenaeans into a goddess-worshipping paradise. Oswald Spengler worked Agamemnon's city into his history of *fin-de-siècle* decadence, *The Decline of the West*. Henry Miller underwent a pacifist epiphany as he communed with Mycenae's belligerent ghosts. With its primitive monumentality and its whiff of totalitarianism, Mycenae was thrillingly *modern*, a site against which the later classical world could begin to seem slightly stuffy and limp-wristed.

While modernity gazed infatuatedly at its own changing reflection in the darkness of Greek prehistory, the excavation of Mycenae continued. The Greek Archaeological Society and the British School of Archaeology in Athens carried on where Schliemann had left off, clearing the acropolis, excavating the town outside the citadel walls and analysing the artefacts. It quickly turned out that most of what Schliemann had claimed for the Tomb of Agamemnon was false: the gold-smothered burials were found to be four centuries too early to have anything to do with the combatants of the Trojan War; the bodies had certainly *not* been interred simultaneously; the nearby house that Schliemann had identified as 'Agamemnon's Palace' was nothing of the sort.

For Schliemann, Mycenae was, above all, the backdrop to Homer. For the archaeologists who succeeded him it was a rather different place. As the site began to be understood more on its own terms, the period sung about by Homer became simply a late phase of a 2000-year-long period of Greek prehistory characterised by the use of weapons and tools made of bronze. The systematic excavation of Mycenae and other similar places allowed archaeologists to piece together the story of the 'Greek Bronze Age', an era of great cultural achievements and social complexity that had grown and flourished only to meet a fiery end sometime around the turn of the twelfth century BC (a couple of generations, in other words, after Herodotus' 1250 BC date for the Trojan conflict).

And thus began a process of splitting off, in which the archaeological consensus about Mycenae became increasingly distant from any popular understanding of the site.

This disjuncture between the chronically garbled versions of Schliemann's Mycenae transmitted by guide books and pop-histories and the highly technical archaeological analysis of Mycenae as a Bronze Age site has resulted in a series of curatorial headaches. How should the material remains of this legendary place be presented to the multitudes who visit the National Archaeological Museum and the ruins of Mycenae every year in vague pursuit of the Tomb of Agamemnon, a monument that doesn't exist?

THE TREASURES OF THE MYCENAEAN WORLD

One thing is certain: no amount of scholarly caution is ever likely to dislodge the Mycenaean shaft-grave gold from its star billing in the most famous museum in Athens. Even from outside the building, as you stand on the wide marble steps leading up to the entrance, the Mask of Agamemnon can be seen (crowds permitting), a smudge of bright gold shining from the centre of the first display case in the 'prehistoric rooms' that occupy the core of the museum. Close up, it is an extraordinarily charismatic artefact, its combination of precious material, startling naturalism and great antiquity, together with the mythic name that is still attached to it, making it stand out as one of the most powerfully compelling archaeological discoveries of all time. A label in the case announces that it is 'known as the mask of Agamemnon', while on the wall a longer information panel explains that this is 'a conventional name, since it is dated 400 years earlier than the Trojan War'. Next to Agamemnon's thin bearded face hangs another gold death mask, this one comically undignified in comparison: a large, round moon, clean-shaven, with fat cheeks, tiny ears and cramped little features.

The back of the same case houses the three other death masks, one round-eyed and smirking, clearly by the same school, if not the same hand, as Agamemnon's moon-faced companion, the other two flat and small with beetling eyebrows and tightly shut eyes. Around the five masks, the rest of the shaft-grave treasure is laid out in all its astonishing profusion. Mycenae's ruling elite were obviously a flashy bunch, preferring to take into the next world a *lot* of gold, vast sheets of the stuff, cut and stamped into dozens of flimsy shapes: diadems that would never stand the rigours of a coronation, breastplates that wouldn't deflect the feeblest Trojan pellet, funereal scales fit to weigh only the lightest soul (illustration 2). Sewn on to the burial clothes of the women were hundreds and hundreds of 'sequins', flat discs, about the circumference of a Rich Tea biscuit but thin as paper, embossed with butterflies, leaves, fish, flowers, stars and spirals. In among all these pretty things it is slightly shocking to come across the gold funeral shrouds of two babies: coverings for the faces, torsos, arms and legs, complete with two lots of tiny gold feet with each toe cut out. Dozens of daggers, swords, cauldrons, cups and vases are arrayed alongside the gold, as well as mysterious votive objects of terracotta, bronze, ivory, wood and crystal.

Behind the famous shaft-grave gold stretches the rest of the Mycenaean collection, a series of beautifully presented displays that divide the long central hall of the museum into smaller rooms. At the back of the first room, somewhat overshadowed by Schliemann's hoard, the finds from another set of shaft graves are displayed. These graves, excavated in 1952, yielded a mere sprinkling of the same thin gold objects, a

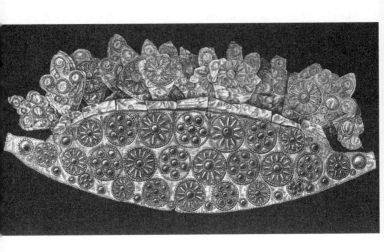

2. One of the funerary ornaments from the third shaft grave, a large crown made, like most of the shaft-grave treasure, of paper-thin gold.

single death mask and this made from dull grey electrum, lots of bronze and terracotta, plus one indisputably gorgeous thing in the form of a rock crystal bowl shaped like a duck.

Beyond these is a room devoted to the palaces of Mycenaean Greece, including two of the most famous arte-facts from Mycenae itself: a large vase with a procession of warriors marching round its circumference, considered by some to be the closest thing we have to a contemporary image of the Greek soldiers going to the Trojan War, and an exquisite ivory carving of two women, kneeling arm in arm, sharing a single shawl, with a toddler clambering over their knees.

The third and last in the series of rooms is filled with the vessels, ritual objects and jewellery that furnished the graves of the rich citizens of Mycenae and the other great Bronze Age cities of Greece, including the sealstones and signet rings on which the artists of the time carved intricate, tiny animals, birds, insects, gods, monsters and scenes of worship. Overall the impression is of great wealth and sophistication, along with a certain ineradicable strangeness. These signet rings, sealstones, weapons, jewels and ritual vessels celebrate the greatness of this king or that queen, their exalted place in a complex universe of beasts and gods and men, in a language that we can never hope fully to understand.

THE RUINS OF MYCENAE

After the National Archaeological Museum, the next stop on the Agamemnon trail is to be found a few hours south-west of Athens in the Peloponnese, the mythical country named for Agamemnon's ancestor Pelops, which reaches its three long fingers into the Aegean Sea. Turning east at a junction on the main artery that links the coastal town of Corinth with its southern neighbour Argos, a long flat road runs through the village of Neo-Mykínes or New Mycenae, a prosperous-looking settlement of warehouse-sized souvenir emporia, campsites and restaurants (illustration 3). The almost symmetrical, cone-shaped peaks of two mountains rear up a couple of kilometres beyond the village, between which, projecting forward out of a deep gorge, is a steep rocky hill crowned with the remains of massive pale-gold stone walls. These are the ruins of the citadel of Mycenae.

A parking area full of coaches and a ticket booth adorned with postcards do little to detract from the remote grandeur of the location. The densely cultivated Plain of Argos, spreading out on three sides of the acropolis, is here a place of vast quiet. With nothing but the wild silence of the mountains behind them and the ordered peace of the groves and fields below, the ruins of Mycenae, perched on their commanding outcrop, retain something of their immemorial charisma. Almost the entire circuit of the walls around the citadel still stands, varying in height from 4 to 7 metres, constructed of enormous stones weighing an average of 2 tonnes. The rock on which they stand thrusts up out of the ground in great slanting striations of hard grey limestone, but so mighty and primordial are the blocks of the city walls that they seem to have been placed there by a force as powerful as the earthquakes that formed the natural landscape. Confronted by these ruins, the Greeks of later centuries explained the monumentality of the walls by attributing them to the Cyclops, a race of giants employed by the city's legendary founder to do the heavy lifting; this

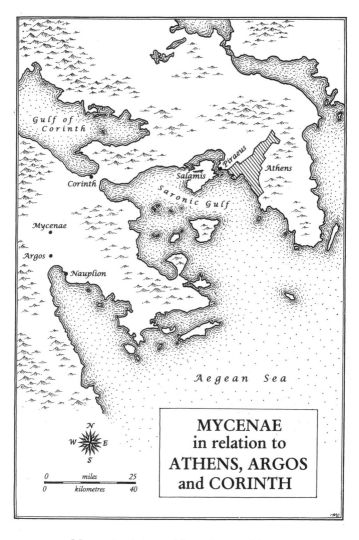

Gulf of
Corinth

Piraeus

Salamis

Athens

Corinth

Saronic
Gulf

Mycenae

Argos

Nauplion

Aegean Sea

MYCENAE
in relation to
ATHENS, ARGOS
and CORINTH

N
W E
S

0   miles   25
0   kilometres   40

3. Mycenae in relation to Athens, Argos and Corinth.

[15]

type of Aegean Bronze Age architecture is still known as 'Cyclopean' (illustration 4).

Shadowed by walls on either side, a broad paved road leads up to the main entrance to the citadel of Mycenae, the famous Lion Gate. Two upright stones form the opening of the gate, supporting an enormous lintel slab. Over the lintel rests a huge triangular piece of the same hard stone, on the face of which two lions, their heads now missing, are carved in low relief. The beasts stand upright facing each other, their front paws resting on the wide plinth of the downward-tapering column that rises between them. The Lion Gate, the earliest extant piece of monumental sculpture in the whole of Europe (dated to 1250 BC), bestows a certain Ozymandias-like melancholy on the landscape, announcing that here was the bastion of a mighty military power over which centuries-long stillness has now descended.

Inside the walls of the citadel, immediately to the right of the Lion Gate, is a large circle, approximately 26 metres in diameter, of tightly fitting vertical stone slabs arranged in two parallel rows a metre apart, roofed in places with a third stone slab. Within the circle about half of the earth has been dug out down to the rock, revealing six rectangular pits, all of different sizes and depths, cut right into the limestone and lined with neat rubble walls. These are the shaft graves where the dazzling array of gold funerary ornaments was found, just as it had been consigned to the earth over 3000 years earlier. The Grave Circle is a remarkably weird monument: much larger and somehow more modern-looking than any other single feature inside the citadel walls, the space that it encloses seems to announce, in all its hallowed uselessness, that here was something of great importance. In its present incarnation

4. Looking over the Cyclopean walls of the citadel of Mycenae towards the fields and groves of the Plain of Argos.

– hunched around a vertiginous archaeological crater – it is almost as much a monument to Heinrich Schliemann's ruthless methods of excavation as it is a memorial of Mycenaean ancestor worship. The long, deep, narrow grave nearest to the Lion Gate was the one that contained the gold Mask of Agamemnon.

Back down the road towards the modern village is the most complete of the ancient structures on the site, the so-called 'Treasury of Atreus'. Fronted by its own ticket booth and car park, the 'Treasury' is, in fact, another royal burial site, one of a series of beehive-shaped chamber tombs that dot the landscape outside the citadel walls. Later in date than the shaft graves, these structures – known as 'tholos' tombs – consist of massive, buried domes, approached by deep passageways cut into the hillsides.

The Treasury of Atreus is by far the largest and grandest of the Mycenaean tholos tombs. Approached by a long walled passageway, the dome itself is entered through a 6-metre high stone doorframe with a lintel slab reputed to weigh 100 tonnes, featuring above it the same 'relieving triangle' as the Lion Gate, this one empty of the ornamental stone panels that would once have filled it. Inside, the steep dome rises to a dizzying 13 metres overhead, each block meticulously engineered to achieve the narrowing circles of the ascending courses of stone. Over the centuries the tomb has been stripped of every decorative element, leaving nothing but the bare structure of its architecture, but not a single stone of the dome is missing. The Treasury's combination of intactness, prehistoric monumentality and absolutely precise engineering is simply astonishing.

There is no other site quite like Mycenae. To understand its uniqueness, consider for a moment the most famous hill in Greece, the Athenian Acropolis. A Bronze Age fortress-city once stood there, and traces of Mycenaean walls are still visible on the lower reaches of the hill beneath the temples. But successive generations of Greek architects dismantled the buildings, levelling the site, re-using the stone and covering up everything that remained. Finally, in the flush of prosperity and self-confidence that followed the Athenian victory over the Persians, the famous temples – the Parthenon, the Erechtheion and the Temple of Athena Nike – were built. Subsequent Roman, Byzantine, Frankish, Venetian and Ottoman accretions were stripped away by Greek nationalists and philhellene archaeologists in the nineteenth century, and now the Acropolis of Athens stands as a monument to just one slice of its rich past, the fifth century BC.

In the north-eastern Peloponnese, near to Mycenae, a similar thing happened. The still-flourishing towns of Argos and Corinth were originally Bronze Age fortresses atop steep peaks, but, just as at Athens, virtually every trace of their heroic history was eradicated by the buildings of later ages. Argos, which lays claim to the longest continuous occupation of any place in Greece, is now the bustling commercial centre of this part of the north-eastern Peloponnese, full of electrical-goods shops, and home on Wednesdays and Saturdays to an enormous open-air market. Its success is easily explained: from almost everywhere that you stand on the fertile soil of the surrounding plain, the cone-shaped acropolis of the city is visible, proudly revealing its effortless topographic superiority. Mycenae, by rather sinister contrast, lurks hidden between two mountains, like a beast of prey waiting to pounce.

Because of its strategically disadvantageous location, Mycenae's mythical splendour is considered something of a mystery. In the Early Bronze Age, stretching for the eight centuries after 3000 BC, Mycenae lagged well behind its better-placed neighbours. The middle period of the Age of Bronze – the six centuries from 2200 to 1600 BC – saw its prosperity beginning slowly to grow, after which its rise was seemingly inexorable. Between about 1600 and 1500 BC – the beginning of the Late Bronze Age – its ever-increasing wealth allowed the royal family to be buried in the shaft graves completely smothered in gold. Their successors built and furnished the splendid beehive tombs. By approximately 1250 BC, Mycenae had grown so much in population and prosperity that the citadel had to be expanded, and it was then that the Lion Gate was erected as a fitting emblem of the city's military and economic power. According to Homer, it had by that time become the dominant city in the whole of Greece. But only a short couple of generations later it was destroyed in a mighty fire, allowing Argos to assume its natural dominance over the fertile plain. Intermittent periods of thin resettlement did little to eradicate the traces of Mycenae's former glory, after which it was completely abandoned.

Mycenae's inexplicable greatness and its abrupt demise have left it as the perfect example of a Bronze Age fortress-city. There are better-preserved contemporary palaces at Pylos, in the western Peloponnese, and Tiryns, a few kilometres south of Mycenae, but neither place has the extensive citadel or the aggressive mountaintop location. The fortress at Gla, although even larger in extent, has none of the legendary reputation. No other Bronze Age site can boast anything equivalent to the Lion Gate, and the Treasury of Atreus is unique in its intactness. Drenched in Homeric glamour and untrammelled by the clutter of modernity, Mycenae stands alone in the landscape, defying the visitor not to be impressed.

THE HERO: LOST AND FOUND AND LOST AGAIN

And impressed they have been. The ruins of Mycenae have dazzled thousands of visitors, filling their imaginations with visions of heroic deeds from Homer and gruesome scenes from the Agamemnon story, stirring the more romantic to extravagant speculation, myth-making and wish-fulfilment. After Schliemann located Agamemnon's tomb, it seemed as though everything had fallen into place: the heroic archaeologist had avenged the hero of antiquity, and the trickle of tourists turned into a flood. But since then the cracks in this account have opened and widened, and the Tomb of Agamemnon is now a wonder of the world made up of a tissue of half-truths, wishful thinking and empty hype, barely papering over the revisions of every part of Schliemann's story. The Homeric epics, once the common heritage of all educated Europeans, have retreated to the margins of academia. These days Mycenae is full of visitors who arrive not quite knowing what it is that they are here to see, who read the guidebook aloud to one another as they look up at the Lion Gate or peer down into the Grave Circle, seemingly still moved, despite their bafflement, by the haunting ruins in their lonely location. And all the while, against the grain of mythical Mycenae, the archaeologists have laboured to piece together an account of

Mycenaean civilisation that fits with the burgeoning material evidence. To them belongs the Museum of Mycenae, an on-site showcase for the latest archaeological consensus, which opened in the summer of 2003.

The museum, built against the north flank of the acropolis below the citadel walls, is a deliberately self-effacing bit of modernism full of discreet quotations from Mycenaean architecture. Against the walls of the marble-floored atrium a series of panels briefly summarises the ancient myths of Mycenae and the history of its excavation; in the middle of the space a three-dimensional scale model of the citadel and surrounding area rests under a glass case.

In the arrangement of the rest of the rooms, the curators seem to have made a virtue of necessity. All the most dramatic and glamorous finds unearthed by archaeologists over the years were spirited away to the National Archaeological Museum in Athens. The site museum contains only the humbler artefacts that stayed behind, plus everything from the recent excavation of the 'Cult Centre', a huddle of buildings just south of the Grave Circle. Few concessions are made to the visitor who wants to situate the glitter of the Athenian displays in the context of the site: as a gentle corrective to such vulgar elitism, the museum guide announces that here 'the brilliance of the gold fades before the human, tangible feel of the clay'. In the room of the site museum dedicated to burials, one case does contain ugly replicas of a few of the shaft-grave items, including, of course, the Mask of Agamemnon, but these are not individually labelled. Moreover, it takes a fairly persistent visitor to winkle anything about the citadel's Grave Circle out of the information panels on the walls, where it is relegated, correctly but austerely, to a late phase of the 'prehistoric cemetery'. So much for the Tomb of Agamemnon.

The Museum of Mycenae succeeds admirably in its aim – to use clay artefacts to present the latest archaeological thinking about Mycenaean culture. But something is lost in the process. There seems to be a paradox at the heart of prehistoric archaeology: the more that is known, the less certainty there can be about any of it. As archaeology becomes more technical, every generalisation crumbles in the face of the complexity of the evidence; as it becomes more sophisticated, self-consciousness strangles speculation in the cradle. At Mycenae, for example, the museum guide is reduced at one point to the bald announcement that the potsherds 'provide incontrovertible evidence for the presence of humans at the site'. But there is more to Mycenae than just the dry kernel of certainty that can be gleaned from an analysis of pottery stratigraphy: the truth about the site must include the layer upon layer of myth that the ruins have attracted over the millennia since its downfall.

The Tomb of Agamemnon may not exist, but it has none the less had a highly productive career, never more so than in the decades after it was supposedly exhumed by an energetic German millionaire. The next five chapters of this book narrate the history of that career, from the 'Cult of the Hero' that sprang up in the ruins of Mycenae in the eighth century BC to the period in the wake of Schliemann's excavations when the Homeric heroes were reinvented to play their part in the tragedies of the twentieth century. This is a story about the power of stories: for twenty-eight centuries the *Iliad* has peopled the ruins of Bronze Age Mycenae with the ghosts of the House of Atreus. Agamemnon was Homer's Lord of

Warlords, and the questions that were asked of him, century upon century, were always about the meaning of war, about hatred and anger and revenge, about murderous competitiveness for resources, about the human spilling of human blood. The Eden of the pagan Greek world was a battlefield, and the cult of Agamemnon's tomb reveals everything about our attitudes towards military power: what does it mean to revere the towering individual who leads his beloved countrymen to death or glory?

In the age of industrialised warfare, after Schliemann told the world he had exhumed the Aryan leader of the Greeks, the answer to that question took a truly nightmarish turn. The last chapter of this book examines the history of the archaeological excavation of the city after the Second World War, sketching the progressively less and less heroic picture of Mycenae that has emerged in the years since 1945. Shocked by the ugliness of the modern ghost of Agamemnon, we have had to reinvent Mycenae once again, as a city without heroes.

2

....

THE CULT OF THE HERO
AND THE AGONY OF WAR

Agamemnon may be absent from the first four rooms of the
Museum of Mycenae, but in the penultimate room Homer's
king of kings makes his belated appearance. The two display
cases that face each other across this small space contain
the material traces of human activity at Mycenae *after* the
Bronze Age, artefacts from those long centuries of ancient
Greek history during which the city stood much as it stands
today, a revered, hero-haunted ruin. Displayed in this room
is a large plate with the name of Agamemnon scratched into
it. Here is a potsherd found at the Grave Circle inscribed 'to
the hero' (illustration 5). Arrayed on these shelves are dozens
of wine cups and figurines, helmets and shields, vases and
swords, just some of the countless offerings left at the city's
two principal shrines. One shrine was sacred to the memory
of Agamemnon; the other was dedicated to the deity in
whose scorched and bloody footprints the hero was destined
always to follow – Ares, the god of war.

So our story of the cult of Agamemnon really begins
here: not during the city's Late Bronze Age heyday, but a
little over 400 years later, when the ruins of the citadel walls
stood higher than anything human-made in the surrounding

5. The Grave Circle of the citadel of Mycenae (Grave Circle A). In the foreground is the entrance, now leading to a precipitous archaeological crater where Schliemann dug up the graves of the Bronze Age Mycenaean kings. A much later potsherd was found here inscribed 'to the hero', suggesting that the spot may have been associated with the Homeric cult.

landscape, attesting to a way of life that had passed away completely. Greece at the start of the eighth century BC was thinly populated, a place of small settlements mostly made of perishable materials; there were no large cities, no writing, no grand stone palaces. The Age of Bronze had been succeeded by the Age of Iron, but the Greek world had yet to exploit the technological potential of the harder, stronger metal. The complex civilisation that produced the citadel of Mycenae – the empire across the seas, the armies and roads, the intricate bureaucracy regulating production and distribution, the community of artists and craftspeople stretching from one end of the known world to the other – had utterly vanished.

As the eighth century wore on, however, Iron Age Greece began to stir; the population was rapidly growing; scattered and unfortified villages began to expand and merge together; the alphabet was making its way westwards from Phoenicia; painters, inspired by a new brilliance in the art of storytelling, started to include human figures among the dense geometric patterns of their pots. Wandering minstrels were arriving at the towns and villages, reciting, along with all the other myths of gods and heroes, two great tales set during and after the Trojan War. These stories represented an unprecedented kind of narrative, unfolding at a slower pace, pivoting round emotions of lust, anger and vengeance recognisable to anyone, yet replete with the vivid physical details of a splendid bygone age. Nearly 3000 years later, in an era bombarded with distractions and amusements of every kind, the *Iliad* can still grab a reader by the throat and not let go until the final, terrible denouement and resolution. In the rather less frivolous Iron Age these epic stories must have provided entertainment of such stupendous power as to make their listeners restless and full of excitement, covetous of glory, dizzy with a nostalgia that was also a sharp goad to action.

At the same time as the Homeric epics were first circulating, groups of aristocrats were leading their followers to found new towns and new colonies. When, in their peregrinations, they came across the traces of the Bronze Age – ruins made of stones so huge that they were surely built by giants under the direction of supermen – they recognised the old tombs and cities sung about by the minstrels. And thus began the practice of Homeric topography. With a reckless abandon that would be repeated at the beginning of the twentieth century, the settlers flung Homeric names about the prehistoric landscape of the Peloponnese. A sort of religious archaeology got underway, in which Bronze Age ruins became the physical setting for a cult of the hero.

Like the gods and the ancestors, heroes were patrons and protectors, granters of success in various undertakings but also sometimes bringers of sickness, barrenness and military defeat. They were remembered, respected, feared and invoked, propitiated by sacrifices, shrines, votive dedications and prayer. At Eleusis, just west of Athens, for example, an anonymous group of Bronze Age graves were identified in the middle of the eighth century BC with the Seven against Thebes – seven legendary generals from Argos who had gone to war against one of the sons of the Theban king Oedipus. The tombs were surrounded with an enclosure wall and became the object of a cult practice that lasted over 800 years. At about the same time, in different parts of Greece, ruling families began to emulate the great funeral rituals of the *Iliad*: the slaughter of animals, offerings of jars of oil, cremation of the dead, quenching of the pyre with wine, placing of ashes in an urn wrapped in cloth, and final heaping-up of a tumulus. All over the Peloponnese offerings were left at Bronze Age ruins, shrines were built in the shadow of the Cyclopean walls, bones dug up and given heroic names.

Appeals to the legendary past served as a way to secure control over tracts of land. If a ruling family could link itself in some way with the hero who had once inhabited a place, its claim to ownership of that locality was greatly enhanced. Aristocratic squatting was thus given a sheen of legitimacy, mellowed by the hastily applied patina of invented tradition. The climax of such a propaganda campaign would be the discovery and display of the physical remains of a hero in the form of a skeleton in a Bronze Age tomb. Sometimes the old burials must have emerged by accident when soil and rubble were being moved for building or a goat put its hoof through the roof of one of the underground beehive tombs; perhaps at other times the digging was deliberate, a search for the bones of the buried heroes so that the finders could pronounce themselves the legitimate guardians and/or descendants of the body.

Heroes filled a niche between gods and mortals rather like that occupied by the Catholic saints: they were venerated through the worship of physical relics and associated with particular places; they had led mortal lives but were possessed of divine powers. But, in keeping with the belligerent purposes to which the hero cult was dedicated, Agamemnon was assuredly no saint. The argument with Achilles that launches the action of the *Iliad* betrays him as selfish, greedy and arrogant, more concerned to slake his lust than to protect the lives of the men under his command. Then, when the consequences of his actions begin to unfold and things start to go really pear-shaped on the battlefield, he wants to turn tail and scurry back to Greece, blaming the gods for tricking him into believing that victory was possible. To compound his crimes, when he finally has to back down and make his peace with Achilles, he refuses to take responsibility for his actions, whining that Zeus had stolen his wits. A hero was prized for power, not virtue; he was worthy of reverence exactly in proportion to his ability to inflict harm upon his enemies. In the case of Agamemnon and Achilles, the bitter damage that was done to the Greek cause by their petty squabble was merely a measure of their greatness.

As the hero cult swept across the Peloponnese, Mycenae became an important centre of this new religious movement. During the five illiterate centuries that had interposed their dark bulk between the Trojan War and the spread of the Homeric epics, Agamemnon's capital had enjoyed an unusual degree of continuity with its heroic past. After it was first sacked and burned in about 1200 BC, the site was reoccupied by a series of settlements that were large enough to keep the stories alive but too humble to build over the ruins. The first of these was a small but thriving town, which lasted about a hundred years until it too was consumed by fire. After a short interval, the acropolis was reoccupied by a huddle of wooden dwellings. For the next three centuries, generations of Greek-speaking, illiterate villagers passed under the Lion Gate on their way in and out of their settlement, and buried their dead among the Bronze Age tombs.

Beginning in about 750 BC, as Greece fell under the spell of the Homeric poems, Mycenae underwent a religious renaissance. Nearly every area that the Bronze Age Mycenaeans had used for burials received offerings. A shrine was constructed near a bridge about a kilometre south of the acropolis, dedicated to Agamemnon. Here the hero was honoured with dedicatory vases and figurines, and appeased by the rising smoke from Homeric-style barbecues. On the road leading north from Mycenae towards Corinth, about a kilometre and a half from the ruins of the citadel, another sanctuary was founded, sacred to Ares, where the god of war was propitiated with weapons and helmets and other military equipment. In the last quarter of the seventh century, on the highest point of the acropolis where the palace had once stood, a temple was built dedicated to the worship of the Homeric goddess Hera.

It is no wonder that the Agamemnon shrine – placed to define the southern edge of Mycenae's territory – was paired in the north with a shrine to brazen Ares, bane of mortals. Throughout their whole turbulent history the Greeks engaged in perpetual war, a way of life that was imbued with religious significance by the unshakeable authority of the *Iliad*. Although the poem purports to narrate an episode of the legendary Trojan War, fought by a unified Greece against a distant enemy, it actually rehearses the predicaments of the warriors of the eighth and seventh centuries in their endless conflicts with their nearest neighbours. Homer's description of the Mycenaeans and the Trojans has the two sides in the conflict speaking the same language, worshipping the same gods, practising the same culture, sharing the same ancestors. He makes little use of the famous legends of the war's pretext – the abduction of Helen – or its conclusion – the ruse of the Trojan horse – and war is thus made to seem like a condition of life without origin, reason or end. The ugliness and brutality of the battlefield are squarely faced – the

Iliad is studded with descriptions of death throes that are clinical in their unflinching detail – but the massing of troops is likened again and again to the great movements of nature: the swarming of insects, the spreading of wildfire, the flight of birds. Homeric man is born into a world governed by war and can do nothing to change it. Individual freedom consists merely in the choice between a hero's glory and a coward's disgrace.

For the Greeks, the battlefield was the ultimate *agon*, probably the single word most symptomatic of the ancient Greek sensibility, meaning a struggle designed or destined to produce a winner and a loser, a rubric that united war with athletic competition, the proceedings of the law-court, the back and forth of rhetorical debate and, indeed, the vicissitudes of fate. Warfare was the most extreme of the arenas in which individual skill and valour joined forces with the favour or displeasure of the gods to decide the latest spin of fortune's wheel. As Heraclitus famously put it: 'War is the father and king of all; and some he has shown as gods, some he has made slaves, others free'.

Indeed, up until a certain point in Greek history, the agony of war *was* somewhat curtailed by the *agon* of warfare. The campaigning season dovetailed with the agricultural cycle. The technology did not exist to storm walled cities and the scale of victory was limited. With a few notable exceptions, conflicts were fought over marginal territories. Even when the individual heroics of aristocratic hand-to-hand combat yielded to the collective style of the hoplites – a citizen-militia manned by heavy infantrymen armed with spears, short swords and wooden shields – conflict among the Greek city-states was conducted according to a set of conventions that tended to limit the bloodshed and economic devastation. Battles were usually set pieces and intended to be decisive. Both forces lined up on a level field, usually in a rough phalanx around eight ranks deep. Common adherence to the hoplite ethic has been called a 'wonderful conspiracy', a ritualistic approach to the *agon* of battle that had the effect of limiting the loss of life.

Then came the fifth century BC. As in our twentieth century, two vast wars cut across the low-level strife, breaking down the conventions of conflict and accelerating the development of technologies of destruction. At the beginning of the century the warring city-states of Greece had to unite against the invading armies of the Persian kings. Outnumbered, the Greeks could not defend themselves by offering the Persians fair fights on level ground. They amassed a great navy under the leadership of Athens and pressed slaves into battle. After their unexpected victory, there was no going back. Instead, the technologies of the Persian Wars were applied to the tradition of competition between Greek city-states with devastating consequences. The wealth of Athens supported 100,000 soldier-slaves and a large navy. An arms race with Sparta ensued. A mere fifty years after the Greeks repulsed the Persian invasion, the Peloponnesian War broke out.

As the foci of a Homeric warrior cult, the shrines of Agamemnon and Ares at Mycenae partook of a strange double life during these world-shattering events. On the one hand Mycenae had been the pre-eminent military power of Homeric legend; on the other hand she was now nothing more than a tiny bit-player in the endless power struggles that raged across the Peloponnese. During the fifth century BC, as Greek warfare increased in scale and destructiveness, Greek historians and dramatists reinvented the Trojan War and Agamemnon's horrible destiny time and again, in an increasingly desperate effort to understand and control their own violent history. During the same period, however, Mycenae itself struggled to maintain even a shred of territorial integrity. Hidden between two peaks and poorly placed for dominance of the plain, she was continually prey to the ambitions of her far more powerful neighbour, Argos. Bronze Age Mycenae, in other words, was to classical Greece what classical Greece would eventually become to nineteenth-century Europe, a place whose ancient history, legendary reputation and symbolic importance stood in poignant contrast to its present political impotence, a place that sometimes seemed to belong to everyone except itself.

At the beginning of the fifth century BC, Mycenae was a small but reasonably secure city-state, protected by its ancient walls, its territory defined to the north and south by its warrior shrines, the citadel dominated by the temple on its highest point, now an elegant stone structure surmounted with a pitched terracotta roof and decorated with relief panels. The city ran its own athletic competition, refereed by officials of the cult of Mycenae's legendary founder, Perseus. It was allied with its neighbour Tiryns, another Bronze Age acropolis sheltering a small population. When the Persian Wars broke out, Mycenae and Tiryns sent a combined contingent of 400 men, which distinguished itself at two decisive battles. At around the same time, perhaps in celebration of the warriors' triumphal return, a temple was established at Mycenae's shrine to Ares, with two columns along its façade, flanked by a separate building equipped for the display of trophies.

But the god of war was shortly to turn his back on his sacred city. In 468 BC, a mere decade after the end of the Persian Wars, Mycenae was sacked by Argos. The Argives laid siege to the city, and the starving Mycenaeans eventually had to surrender, whereupon the victors dismantled various key sections of the citadel walls and sold its inhabitants into slavery. There are various reasons given for this murderous bit of neighbourly spite: one writer has Argos jealous of the Mycenaean valour in the Persian Wars (the Argives themselves had pursued a policy of neutrality); another historian advances the theory that the two cities had quarrelled about the administration of the mini-Olympics of the north-eastern Peloponnese, the Nemean Games. Whatever the reason, in the classical period that followed the Greek victory over Persia, Mycenae was once again deserted, brought down by that same brutal internecine Peloponnesian competitiveness that would eventually bring even Athens to her knees.

Mycenae may have been stomped on by Argos, but its past glories had never seemed more significant. Herodotus – the Greek from the western coast of modern Turkey whose account of the Persian Wars garnered for himself the title of the 'father of history' – opened his narrative with a recap of Greco-Persian relations since the earliest times. This seemed mainly to consist of the tit-for-tat abduction of various princesses. But when it came to Paris carrying off Helen, he recounts, the Greeks broke the tacit agreement that a woman was not worth going to war over and went ahead and burned Troy. Later Herodotus tells how the Persian king Xerxes, on his way to invade Greece, climbed the ruins of Troy and made a sacrifice of 1000 oxen on the acropolis, swearing to avenge the Trojan heroes. For both sides in the Persian Wars,

Agamemnon's Trojan campaign was reinvented as a precursor to the conflict, deployed by the Persians as the pretext for aggression and brandished by the Greeks as the prefiguration of victory.

Agamemnon and his family also enjoyed a very high cultural profile in fifth-century Athens, starring in one after another of the tragedies that were staged every year as part of a spring festival held in honour of the god Dionysus. The festival featured a competition between plays, a series of one-off performances judged by a panel of citizens representing the people of Athens. These performances – the *agon* of tragedy – were far more than works of art in the modern sense. For the Greeks, the meaning of the world revealed itself through its stories, and the artists who best retold those stories wielded a cultural influence without parallel in the modern world. Victorious playwrights were legal theorists, theologians and political philosophers, civic teachers who worked out, through the action of gods and men in their plays, the legal and ethical questions raised by the democratic experiment. And of all the stock of legends from which the tragedians wrought their art, the curse of the House of Atreus was the most often recycled.

The most important of the treatments of the Agamemnon story was also the earliest (or at least the earliest that has survived) penned by Aeschylus, an aristocratic veteran of the Persian Wars who began to write plays as a young man, producing a string of hits in early middle age, and who was said to have been killed, in Sicily, at the age of 69, by an eagle who dropped a tortoise on his head. In Aeschylus' Agamemnon trilogy, *the Oresteia*, the legends' murderous pendulum of anger and retribution is presented as a series of puzzles about the relationship between justice and vengeance. The first of the plays, the *Agamemnon*, tells the story of the Mycenaean king's return from Troy and his murder by his unfaithful wife. In Aeschylus' version it is Clytemnestra who engineers the whole thing, first tricking Agamemnon into walking on a cloth of sacred purple – an act of hubris which she hopes will anger the gods – then trussing him up in a dressing-gown-cum-straightjacket and stabbing him in his bath. The next two plays, the *Choephori* and the *Eumenides*, pivot around the figure of Orestes, the unfortunate young man whose job it is to kill his mother in vengeance for his father's murder. The *Choephori* chronicles the grisly deed itself. In the *Eumenides* the family curse is finally laid to rest by a decision of a jury of twelve Athenians, convened by Athena, who try Orestes for the murder of his mother and, after Athena casts the deciding vote, exonerate him. The trilogy ends on a celebratory note, the stage filled with revellers.

It is in his confecting a happy ending to the curse of the House of Atreus that Aeschylus projects most blatantly the political and legal dilemmas of his own time back to the distant past. The divine court that decides Orestes' fate would have been immediately recognisable to his audience as the Areopagus, the Athenian equivalent of the House of Lords, a judicial and political body whose members were recruited from the ruling classes of Athens and held their posts for life. Like the House of Lords, it tended towards conservatism, and four years before the first production of the *Oresteia* a radical element in the Athenian Assembly had gained the upper hand and decided to strip this body of most of its powers, except that of jurisdiction in cases of homicide. By asserting that this institution was founded by Athena herself for the purpose of trying Orestes for the murder of his mother, the playwright gave this spanking new political compromise an ancient and divine origin, enshrining it in both art and theology.

The radical reforms that stripped the Areopagus of many of its powers had a foreign policy aspect, involving none other than Mycenae's old rival Argos. The reformist faction had risen to power in the wake of a disastrous expedition by the conservatives to aid their Peloponnesian ally Sparta. Sparta rejected their aid, and the conservatives returned humiliated. The radicals promptly seized their chance and pushed through their programme of reform, including dumping the Spartans and embracing Argos as their new ally. Aeschylus, cleaving closely to the new alignments of power, chose to crown this achievement with another politically expedient anachronism, depriving Mycenae of its Homeric renown by setting his Agamemnon trilogy in Argos instead. In a creepy bit of Orwellian Newspeak, Aeschylus' Apollo tells Athena that he has sent Orestes to Athens 'to make your city great', promising that 'He and his city shall forever be your faithful allies.' An alliance that was a mere four years old was made to seem as ancient as the Trojan War. Now for Aeschylus' audience it was their new ally Argos who led the Greeks to Troy in the past and who would follow Athens to glory in the future. The humiliation of Mycenae was complete.

Making an enemy of Sparta was, of course, Athens' downfall. As the fifth century BC drew to a close, the Spartans finally succeeded in their twenty-five-year quest to destroy the Long Walls that connected Athens with her seaport at Piraeus. In 405 BC the Long Walls were dismantled, and a pro-Spartan oligarchy of thirty tyrants was imposed on the city. Mycenae, deserted since it had been sacked by Argos, as if in anticipation of the self-destruction of the rest of classical Greece, now stood as a symbol of loss and ruin. In the opening passages of his *History of the Peloponnesian War*, Thucydides ponders the wreckage of Mycenae, assimilating Agamemnon's war record into a brief history of Hellenic conflict from the earliest times. Child of the Athenian experiment in democracy, Thucydides had little time for heroic nostalgia. His Mycenae is small and primitive; his Agamemnon only a couple of generations away from total barbarism. Stripped of its poetry, the story is a stark one, and the severely rationalistic Thucydides does not shrink from narrating it as such. Dismissing the pretext of the abduction of Helen as poetic fancy, Thucydides flatly avers that it was Agamemnon's superiority in strength, rather than widespread adoration of the beautiful Helen, which had enabled the king of kings to unite the Greeks.

On the Athenian stage, too, Agamemnon fared badly during the Peloponnesian War. Euripides, the last of the great trio of tragedians, chose to represent the legendary campaign against Troy from the point of view of the vanquished, and his *Trojan Women* amounts to a furious polemic against the very concept of victory. The action of the play takes place in front of the smoking ruins of Troy, where the captive women are being held by the Greeks pending their departure. As they prepare to leave their homeland for a life of slavery, the news comes through of who will be assigned to which master. It emerges that Agamemnon has taken a fancy to Cassandra, the royal daughter of Priam and Hecuba, who has been endowed with the gift of prophecy by Apollo but doomed by the same god never to be believed. Soon after this announcement, Cassandra bursts on to the stage carrying a torch in

each hand and singing a defiant song of joy at the impending sacrifice of her virginity to the enemy king. She alone
knows the horrible fate that awaits all the Greeks, including the murder of Agamemnon by Clytemnestra. Everyone
on stage regards her behaviour as completely deranged but
the audience, aware of the truth of her prophecy, appreciates
the harsh logic of her euphoria. The Athenian optimism that
saw Aeschylus *resolve* Agamemnon's family curse had now
been usurped by the most bitter pessimism. For Euripides,
the moral of the legend of the House of Atreus is that war
can have no true winners.

But in defiance of any efforts to understand, control or
prevent war, the endless fighting that fuelled but also consumed and destroyed Greek civilisation continued almost
without a break. After the Peloponnesian War, Spartan
hegemony flickered and waned, compromised by the deal
Sparta had to broker with the Persians, undermined by the
reconquest of Athens by the exiled democrats, and then
swept away by the mainland city of Thebes. Theban domination was short lived, ending with the death of her field com-
mander, but the Theban way of war had been passed on to
the king of a hitherto obscure and backward state, Philip of
Macedon, who promptly conquered Thebes and Athens and
moved against Persia. Upon his assassination, his 20-year-
old son Alexander inherited his machinery of conquest and
used it to create the largest empire the world had ever seen,
stretching from Italy to India, bringing in the wake of his
armies the culture of Hellenistic Greece.

In between these large-scale conflicts, the tide of world
war would ebb only to expose the dreary peaks of the
Peloponnese still locked in their constant feuding. The antag-

onism between Argos and Mycenae took another twist early in the third century BC, when Hellenistic Argos, in need of a military base to defend its northern frontier against various enemies, established a fortified outpost at Mycenae, repairing the walls that it had so carefully dismantled a century and a half earlier. Of all the periods of reoccupation of Mycenae, this one was the most extensive. The Argives enclosed the lower town, built another temple on the foundations of the sixth-century BC one, constructed a fountain house and a theatre and covered the acropolis in neat rows of houses. Mycenae was now nothing more than an annexe of Argos, its first line of defence against the aggression of its northern neighbours.

This was a time of relentless instability: the Achaean League waged war on the Argive tyrants, the Spartans fought everybody, the boundaries between the territories of different factions on the Peloponnese fluctuated wildly. The Argives bolstered their courage in these endless conflicts by refurbishing the belligerent sanctuaries at Mycenae. The Agamemnon shrine was cleaned up, the structure roofed and the floor paved. The Ares sanctuary was rebuilt once again and received, among other objects, the offering of a large bronze shield inscribed with the words 'From the Argives … to the Gods … from the spoils of King Pyrrhus' (the Epirote king whose costly successes against the Romans entered the language as the term 'Pyrrhic victory').

In the middle of the second century BC, however, the agonistic spirit of the Peloponnese was at last absorbed and subdued by the *pax Romana*. At around this time, Mycenae, having outlived its usefulness as a shrine to the heroes and gods of war, was finally abandoned, never to be reoccupied except by a scattering of shepherds or a few squatters, availing themselves of the ever-flowing spring above the old citadel (still to be seen quenching the thirst of sheep and goats on the hillside behind the ruins).

The city appears once more in the written record of antiquity. In the middle of the second century AD, by which time Greece was a culturally prestigious but politically impotent province of the Roman empire, one of the unlikeliest immortals of ancient literature made the pilgrimage to Mycenae. Pausanias, a Greek-speaking native of the west coast of what is now Turkey, undertook to produce a comprehensive guide to the monuments and remains of Greece, a massive project that eventually ran to ten volumes. It is its artistic shortcomings that make Pausanias' *Description of Greece* so invaluable. Written in an unembellished style, and following a pedantic topographical system in which he marched into the capital of each province, made an exhaustive tour of the town beginning in the centre and then followed in turn each one of its radiating roads out to the edges of the district describing everything of note that he passed, his guidebook has led generations of curious modern travellers through the complex landscape of ancient Greece.

Greece under the Roman empire was saturated in nostalgia for a series of lost golden ages, an atmosphere in which tourism flourished. Accordingly, Pausanias appears to regard the purpose and value of his work as completely self-evident and does not bother with a preface, plunging baldly into an account of sailing past Cape Sunium on the way to the Piraeus. A tour of Athens and Attica takes up the whole of the first volume, and the second book begins with his descent into the Peloponnese. On the road between Corinth and Argos he announces, as though intoning into a microphone on a tour-bus, 'we have on the left the ruins of Mycenae'. After narrating at rather tedious length the myths of Mycenae's founding and mentioning its fifth-century BC destruction by Argos, he comments tersely on what can still be seen of the city: parts of the circuit walls and the Lion Gate 'said to be the work of the Cyclops …'.

Somewhere on the approach to the ruins Pausanias seems to have been collared by one of the garrulous guides who eked out a precarious living by pouncing on travellers as they wandered along the heritage trail. One way or another he was shown the highpoints of the remains of Mycenae. First he visited the 'underground buildings of Atreus and his children, where their treasures were kept'. These must have been the beehive tombs outside the citadel, which acquired their reputation as treasuries from the stories of the splendid grave goods plundered from them over the centuries, and it is only because of the abiding usefulness of Pausanias' books that the Treasury of Atreus is still called by that name. By the second century AD they would presumably have long been empty, and it is not clear from his account whether he was actually able to enter any of them (illustration 6).

The guide then took Pausanias to an unspecified location where he was shown the Tomb of Agamemnon. The long existence of a *shrine* to Agamemnon far outside the citadel walls suggests that the tomb of the king may have not been identified with any particular spot until after Mycenae was abandoned. Was it only when the Agamemnon and Ares shrines fell into disuse that somewhere on the site was identified with the burial place of the Homeric hero? It seems quite likely that Pausanias was taken inside the citadel and shown the Grave Circle with its five tombstones enclosed

6. The entrance to the so-called 'Treasury of Atreus'. The mistaken identification of these beehive tombs with kingly strong-rooms originates with Pausanias, who was shown them as such in the second century AD by a tour guide.

in a double ring of thin grey slabs, although it is hard to say why the monument might have reappeared at this late point in Mycenae's history. Maybe an entrepreneurial tour guide or reverential Homeric scholar organised the excavation of parts of the ruins. A more plausible, if less appealing explanation is that some stones were removed for building and it appeared by accident.

Wherever it was that Pausanias was shown as marking the spot, the tradition of the Tomb of Agamemnon was clearly flourishing, and he goes on to list various members of the warlord's retinue who were murdered and buried alongside him, including the captured Trojan princess Cassandra, Agamemnon's charioteer Eurymedon and 'Teledamus and Pelops ... said to have been the twin children of Cassandra, who were murdered by Aegisthus after he had murdered their parents'. (These twin boys, bastard offspring of Cassandra and Agamemnon, would enjoy a late-blooming celebrity after Schliemann's excavation of their pathetic little golden shrouds.) As for the murderers themselves, Pausanias rounds off his account of Mycenae by asserting that 'Clytemnestra and Aegisthus were buried at a little distance from the wall; for they were deemed unworthy to be buried within the walls, where Agamemnon himself and those who had been murdered with him were laid.'

And there Pausanias stops, recording nothing of his impressions of the ruins of the city: if he went inside the Treasury of Atreus, he did not comment on its magnificent architecture; if he was awed or disappointed by the citadel walls and the Lion Gate he does not let on. This does not mean that he was immune to the grandeur of Bronze Age remains: he greets the walls of Tiryns – 'made of unwrought

[45]

stones, each stone so large that a pair of mules could not even stir the smallest of them' – with a passionate eulogy, ticking off the Greeks for admiring the Egyptian pyramids while ignoring their own equally magnificent antiquities. But Mycenae, by contrast, seems too overwhelmed by its legendary reputation for Pausanias to react to it with any immediacy. For our Greco-Roman tour guide these pale-gold stones were little more than pegs to hang myths on.

3

....

MYCENAE ENLIGHTENED

After Pausanias a millennium and a half of silence fell over the ruins of Mycenae. In the fourth century AD, after Constantinople had become the spiritual and administrative centre of the new Christian empire of Byzantium, Greece was aggressively 'depaganised', the oracle of Delphi forcibly closed, the Olympic Games discontinued. Christian Byzantium had no need of pagan heroes such as Agamemnon, and his famous city, tucked into its remote corner of the Plain of Argos, first faded from the cultural map and then physically disappeared as the Lion Gate, the Grave Circle and much of the circuit of walls were buried by mud and debris washed down from the higher reaches of the acropolis by centuries of winter rain.

In the Middle Ages Greece became a provincial backwater of the Byzantine empire, burdened by a top-heavy imperial administration, split into semi-autonomous provinces ruled by generals and vulnerable to wave upon wave of invaders. For 200 years or so Franks, Venetians, Genoese and Catalans fought over her soil, eventually all succumbing to the extraordinarily efficient military machinery of the Ottoman empire, the Muslim superpower that had taken Constantinople in 1453. During this period the steep hills of the north-eastern Peloponnese took on something of their Bronze Age aspect as the Franks, the Venetians and then the Turks all built fortresses on the peaks of Corinth, Nauplion and Argos. Mycenae, as poorly located for domination of the Argolid as ever, was passed over in this spate of belligerent architectural activity. In 1700, however, during one of the intermittent bouts of war between the Turks and the Venetians, an enterprising Venetian engineer, scouring the locality for stone with which to build the massive fortress that still stands on the Palamidi rock in Nauplion, started to dismantle the debris, uncovering the Lion Gate. Mycenae had reappeared.

The reappearance of Agamemnon's capital in the first year of the eighteenth century coincided with a new enthusiasm for Homer in northern Europe, and a gradual expansion in the market for the antiquities of pagan Greece. French and British agents began to comb the country for bits and pieces with which to adorn their clients' châteaux and stately homes, channelling the two nations' long-standing power struggle into an extended bout of competitive plunder. Both countries justified their activities with the claim that civilisation had fled Greece and found a new abode in colder climes. By giving rein to their acquisitiveness, so the argument went, they were merely saving Europe's classical heritage from the dangerous bandits, ignorant peasants and wily Turks who made up the contemporary inhabitants of the lands of legend.

One of the earliest northern European travellers to leave a record of his visit to Mycenae was a French clergyman, Michel Fourmont, who had accepted a commission from a minister of Louis XV to 'obtain for the library of the king everything that can be found in the Levant, in the form of Greek manuscripts or books written in the different oriental languages'. In 1728 Fourmont spent sixteen months in Greece, during which time he visited Mycenae and made some drawings of the walls and the gate. Luckily, the sheer antiquity of Agamemnon's city saved it from the excesses of the cleric's tornado approach to antiquarian research. Writing home to the French officials who directed his activities, Fourmont described how he hired local workmen to demolish any structures whose walls might be a source of inscriptions. At Sparta he bragged that he 'overturned it from top to bottom and there isn't one stone left on top of another'. Mycenae was spared this treatment only by virtue of the fact that it was prehistoric – too monumental to haul bits away and too ancient to provide inscriptions.

The fashion for pagan antiquities spread from France to England, and in 1734, a few years after Fourmont's rapacious tour of the Peloponnese, the Society of Dilettanti was founded by 'some gentlemen who had travelled in Italy, desirous of encouraging at home a taste for those objects which had contributed so much for their entertainment abroad'. Extravagantly bibulous dinners gave the Dilettanti a reputation for frivolity – Horace Walpole waspishly remarked that it was a 'club, for which the nominal qualification is having been in Italy, and the real one, being drunk' – but the Society numbered among its members many genuine enthusiasts and serious antiquarians. Until the end of the eighteenth century, the itinerary of a Dilettanti Society Grand Tour consisted of France, Italy, Germany and Switzerland, but when, in 1796, Napoleon's armies occupied Italy, the Society had to be diverted to a new destination. As the century turned, a few of the more committed members began to brave the dangers and discomforts of the 'Near East', as Ottoman Greece was then known.

The Dilettanti who visited Mycenae clambered around

the Lion Gate and the Treasury of Atreus equipped with the tools of Enlightenment standardisation: the sextant, the measuring rule, the camera obscura and the surveyor's plane table. Touring Greece with Pausanias in one hand and Homer in the other, these travellers followed the same circumscribed routes through the perils of Greece to the citadel of Mycenae, diligently consuming and repeating each other's measurements and quoting the same bits of the same classical texts. This resulted in rather repetitive descriptions of the legendary city, despite the often self-congratulatory sense of individual adventure with which these young men galloped up to the Lion Gate. Poetry and pedantry meshed seamlessly in their approach to ancient topography. Mycenae was shivered over as the ultimate romantic ruin, but it was also described, illustrated, analysed, mapped and measured as an object of scientific curiosity.

Of all the Dilettanti who toured Greece at the turn of the nineteenth century, none was more passionate about the Peloponnese than Edward Dodwell, a scholar and artist who quit Trinity College Cambridge in 1800 when he was in his early thirties and devoted much of the rest of his life to researching 'Cyclopian remains'. In the preface to his posthumously published *Views and Descriptions of Cyclopian, or Pelasgic Remains* Dodwell was cast as the Bronze Age's first modern martyr who had 'never completely recovered from a severe illness brought on by great fatigue and long exposure to the sun in the summer of 1830, when seeking for the situation of some ancient cities …'. His reverence for Mycenae was unbounded, and he wrote of approaching it 'with a greater degree of veneration than any other place in Greece had inspired. Its remote antiquity, enveloped in the deepest recesses of recorded time, and its present extraordinary remains, combined to fill my mind with a sentiment in which awe was mingled with admiration.' He decided that the Lion Gate looked Egyptian, that the Treasury of Atreus was probably a sepulchre, and that the Tomb of Agamemnon would be found within the confines of the lower town rather than on the citadel. 'There is no place in Greece', he concluded, 'where a regular and extensive plan of excavation might be prosecuted with more probable advantage, or where remains of greater interest and a higher antiquity might be brought to light' (illustration 7).

The notorious Lord Elgin was in Greece at the same time as Dodwell, the latter witnessing with anguish the former's dismantling of the Parthenon frieze. Mycenae did not escape Elgin's attentions and he engaged his faithful archaeological sidekick, the British embassy chaplain Philip Hunt, to scope it out, receiving in 1801 a mouth-watering report of the Treasury of Atreus, 'a most stupendous conical subterranean building, quite entire, called by some the Tomb of Agamemnon, by others the Royal Treasury of Mycenae'. (The designation of this beehive tomb as a 'treasury' originated, as mentioned above, with Pausanias. Because it is second only to the Lion Gate as the most impressive architectural feature of the site, it has also frequently been identified as Agamemnon's resting place. This jumble of titles attests to the confusions that have always resulted from trying to make the visible remains of Mycenae fit with the city of legend.)

In 1802 Elgin visited Mycenae with his wife, who wrote home to her mother that she had had to crawl *on all fours* through the relieving triangle above the door to enter the Treasury, where she found herself in 'an immense hollowed

7. Detail of Edward Dodwell's engraving of the interior of the Treasury of
Atreus showing the state of the monument in the early nineteenth century.
The few missing stones to the right of the relieving triangle above the
entrance have since been identified and replaced. Dodwell has exaggerated
the scale of the tomb by making the people much too small, standard
Romantic shorthand for the sublimity of antiquity.

sugar loaf … composed of hewn stone'. Having thus domesticated the most impressive monument of prehistoric Greece, the Elgin party swept off on a series of 'superbly caparisoned' horses provided by the Turkish governor of Argos, stayed in a house in town which he had furnished for their reception, and quit Argos the next day leaving instructions with their host to organise the excavation of the Treasury. Returning six days later they found the doorway cleared, and were shown some fragments of vases and ornamental stonework, along with some pieces of a marble fluted vase, all of which they carted off with them. Again, the prehistoric monumentality of the site saved it from the worse excesses of aristocratic acquisitiveness: Philip Hunt commented that 'having admired the two lions over the gate, [Elgin] felt very sorry that their transportation made impossible their removal' (illustration 8).

In 1809 the same unholy alliance of British aristocracy and Ottoman officialdom saw the further excavation of the Treasury of Atreus, when the second Marquis of Sligo joined with the Pasha of Nauplion to clear the monument. This time large sections of the half-columns of intricately carved, hard green limestone that flanked the doorway, plus a number of other fragments of decorative stonework, were shipped back to England, then transported by the marquis to the family seat in County Mayo in Ireland. There they languished, unappreciated, for nearly a century, until the fifth marquis happened to read an account of his ancestor's excavation and went on a hunt through the estate for its fruits. In 1905 he presented the fragments to the British Museum. Two restored columns incorporating the original pieces now grace the entrance to the antiquities department on the ground

8. The Lion Gate, the main entrance to the citadel of Mycenae. This is the earliest example of monumental sculpture in the whole of Europe that can still be viewed in its original setting. Lord Elgin wanted to dismantle the Lion Gate and take it off to London along with the Parthenon frieze but luckily for Mycenae it was too big to ship.

floor of the museum, giving a good sense of the sheer scale of the tomb that they once adorned.

The fact that Mycenae was more or less unchanged since Pausanias' day was remarked by one after another of the travellers. Colonel William Leake, a British army officer who surveyed the Peloponnese with unflagging energy and unprecedented precision, marvelled over the fact that 'everything left at Mycenae dates from the heroic age; and notwithstanding this remote antiquity, the description of Pausanias shews that Mycenae has undergone less change since he travelled than any place in Greece'. Peter Laurent, who swanned around Greece, Turkey and Italy tut-tutting at the impertinence of the natives, echoes Leake's sentiment: 'nothing but ruins have remained of this city for the last two thousand three hundred and eighty-seven years, and those which modern travellers have once more discovered are, with little difference, the same as those described by Pausanias …'. A detail of Laurent's account is eloquent of the aristocratic texture of these amateur antiquarian researches when he records that a cistern on the citadel is 'covered in the interior with a sort of hard plaster on which the point of a sabre makes but little impression'. The most unromantic account of Mycenae from this period is bequeathed by a fellow of Trinity College Cambridge, William Clark, who takes his cue from Thucydides and warns against being 'deluded by the genius of ancient poets' into thinking that Mycenae is anything more than 'a little nest on a ledge of barren rock'.

In 1806 the French author François René de Chateaubriand went off in search of the combined Hellenic and Christian roots of European civilisation, travelling from Paris to Jerusalem via Greece. Out of a ten-month tour, only nineteen days were spent in Greece, and his tour of Mycenae was of necessity rather perfunctory. Despite his evident desire to stamp the impress of his personality on all his descriptions of the landscape of modern Greece, even Chateaubriand did not escape the unvarying catalogue of the wonders of the site and the same rehearsal of excerpts from Pausanias to be found in all the accounts of the time. He described how he first visited the Treasury of Atreus (for Chateaubriand, the 'tombeau d'Agamemnon'), then rode his horse up the flank of a hill to admire the 'colossal' lions on the gate, comparing them to Egyptian sculpture. After this whirlwind tour, Chateaubriand set off once again for the road to Corinth, only to put his foot right into the vault of another beehive tomb. Citing Pausanias, he decided that he had stumbled upon the extramural burial place of Agamemnon's assassins, exclaiming over the 'singular destiny' that saw him leave Paris only to discover the 'ashes of Clytemnestra'. This mythic turn of events could not detain him for long, however, and the next sentence finds our hero arriving in Corinth in plenty of time for dinner.

Nationalism was as important a part of the Enlightenment tool-box as any measuring instrument, and Mycenae's increasing visibility over the course of the early nineteenth century was entangled with the emergence of Greece as a modern nation-state. The gradual uncovering and measuring of the ruins accompanied by repeated invocations of Homer and Pausanias represented a symbolic reclamation of the monument from the Ottomans. Even as the Dilettanti and their fellow travellers were exclaiming over the neglected tombs of ancient Hellenic heroes, rebellions on the western fringes of the Sultan's territories were softening the ground for another stab at liberation on the part of the modern Greeks. In 1821 the Peloponnese exploded into war. Demand for Peloponnesian travel memoirs was given a great boost by the outbreak of the Greek War of Independence, and the wonders of Mycenae found an ever-wider audience as one Dilettante after another rushed into print with an account of his wanderings.

By 1822 the insurgents had control of the Peloponnese, had adopted a constitution and had begun to fight among themselves. While the Greeks quarrelled, their military situation worsened. The Sultan found a new ally in the ruler of Egypt, took control of Crete, and began to go after the Peloponnesian rebels. The Greeks appealed once more to the Great Powers, who had steadfastly refused to intervene against the Ottomans. By 1825, however, with their trading interests affected by the war and paranoid lest one of their number turn the conflict to its own advantage, they were more inclined to get involved. Entering into a cautious pact, Britain, France and Russia agreed to join the hostilities, and sent a naval flotilla to the Peloponnese. In 1826 the ships turned their far superior gunpower on to the Turkish fleet at the battle of Navarino, effectively bringing the war to an end. It was symptomatic of the political dependence of the new nation that the Greeks themselves were not party to the 1832 pact that put a young Bavarian prince on the throne. Prince Otto was a fitting symbol of the ironies of Greek nationalism, being the son of King Ludwig, the Bavarian philhellene who had caused Munich to be rebuilt in the sanitised image of fifth-century BC Athens.

In 1828, in the wake of the victory at Navarino, a detachment of French troops was shipped over to the Peloponnese, accompanied by the members of a scientific expedition. This included geologists, meteorologists, topographers, botanists, zoologists and, of course, archaeologists, eager to locate the Peloponnese on the grid of Linnaean classification and in the axes of Cartesian space. Despite the protestations of the archaeologist Abel Blouet that Mycenae presented the most extraordinary ancient ruins to be found anywhere in the world, resembling nothing else in Greece, the drawings of the city produced by the expedition and published in 1834 tamed it into a vision of enlightenment rationality.

Immediately after the War of Independence, Mycenae's location in the romantic-nationalist heart of post-Ottoman Europe made it a convenient symbol either of revolution or of monarchical counter-revolution, depending on the political tastes of the visitor. In 1840 the ardent French royalist J. A. Buchon toured the Peloponnese in pursuit of the Frankish settlers of the Middle Ages, a group, according to his nostalgic historiography, of chivalrous knights, beautiful chatelaines and singing shepherds who had 'founded their Baronies in the same valleys where the Homeric kings had prospered'. Buchon found Mycenae 'perfect' and 'charming'. The sight of the citadel triggered opposing sentiments in the breast of the Polish poet Juliusz Słowacki, who travelled in the Peloponnese in 1836 and included his impressions of 'Agamemnon's Tomb' in his long, digressive poem 'Journey to the Holy Land from Naples'. The verses begin 'Oh, Poland!' and consist of a rant, only tenuously tethered to Greek mythology, about the political impotence of the poet's fatherland, then languishing under the Russian yoke.

For the Greeks themselves, independence brought with it the burdens and rewards of a heritage industry. On 28 April 1837 the Greek Archaeological Society held their first meeting on the Parthenon, pledging themselves to the 'discovery, recovery and restoration of antiquities in Greece'. In 1841 the Society finally cleared the whole approach to the Lion Gate under the supervision of one of its founders, the tireless Kyriakos Pittakes, whose bulldog-like dedication to the cause of national heritage managed partially to stem the steady flow of antiquities out of the country.

Archaeology may have been symbolically important to the new Greek nation, but excavation is an expensive business; the Society was in perpetual financial crisis and many promising sites – attested to in ancient literature, and liberally strewn with visible remains – were perforce left undug. Into this opportunity a fabulously wealthy German merchant elbowed himself in the 1870s, undertaking at his own expense the first in-depth archaeological excavation of Mycenae. A self-made millionaire who devoted the second half of his life and much of his enormous fortune to excavating the sites of Homeric legend, Heinrich Schliemann has featured in popular history as the reincarnation of a character from Homer, a larger-than-life figure whose extraordinary energy, unflagging sense of purpose and god-given luck led him to find the very objects mentioned in the epic poetry of ancient Greece.

4

....

AGAMEMNON AWAKENED

The First Cemetery in Athens is a splendid affair, a huge site sprawling over a few acres just to the south-east of the city centre, replete with monuments of staggering grandeur and self-importance. The predominance of the neo-classical style for remembering the dead of Athens makes of the First Cemetery a rather less overwhelmingly Christian experience than other cemeteries in Greece, more like a miniature pastiche of a classical city, with columns outnumbering crosses. But among the memorials, none is more wholeheartedly pagan than the mausoleum to Heinrich Schliemann that rears up at the front of a steep ridge just to the left as you enter the cemetery. The mausoleum itself is a monumental marble building with a bronze door decorated with spiral motifs taken from the stonework of a Bronze Age tomb. This is surmounted by a miniature classical temple in white marble, at the front of which a bust of Schliemann, complete with drooping moustache, frowns at the splendid distant view of the Parthenon to be had from this spot (illustration 9).

Around the base of the temple is a frieze, sculpted in the same glittering white stone, depicting a whole cycle of archaeological heroism, from the building of the Cyclopean walls thousands of years ago to their excavation in the 1870s. The scene on the west segment, the first in the series, shows

9. Schliemann frowning at the Parthenon from his prime location in the First Cemetery in Athens. The frieze below the bust on this neo-Homeric tomb depicts the building of the Cyclopean walls of Tiryns, and a Greek inscription above it reads 'To Schliemann the Hero'.

King Proteus directing not the one-eyed giants of myth, but some muscular, nearly-naked slaves as they shape the stones for the walls of Tiryns. On the south side are scenes from Agamemnon's story, ending with Orestes making an offering at his tomb. The east side features a parallel series of scenes from the *Odyssey*. The final section of frieze shows the excavations of Mycenae and Troy, beginning with the removal of stones in front of the Lion Gate and ending with the hauling away of a cart-load of goodies from Troy. Schliemann and his wife stand in the middle, directing the action. Above Schliemann's bust a Greek inscription reads 'To Schliemann the Hero', and below the Tiryns frieze a couplet reads: 'I cover Heinrich Schliemann of great renown. You should imitate him; he laboured hard for mortals'.

Schliemann himself composed the heroic inscriptions on his tomb; he was a great self-mythologiser, a man whose knack for turning out an appealing story about his life was as unfailing as his nose for a good business opportunity. Many later biographers were only too willing to cash in on Schliemann's skill in this regard, building on and further exaggerating his own account of his exploits. The apotheosis of this tradition must be the trashy hagiography by the German pop historian of archaeology Hans Baumann, which was first published in Germany in 1966 and later translated and published (by none other than the highly respectable Oxford University Press) in England under the title *Lion Gate and Labyrinth*. By doggedly embroidering every one of Schliemann's stories, Baumann ended up with a syrupy blend of Homer and Hollywood very true to the spirit of Schliemann's own self-fashioning. The first chapter, entitled 'Odysseus comes home', opens with Schliemann (a native of north-eastern Germany) in a frail barque on the way to Odysseus' island: 'His eyes were fixed on Ithaca all day, and when night fell, he held his gaze as steadily as a man who is returning home.' The chapter ends with a touching encounter with a Greek farmer who hails Schliemann as 'indeed an Odysseus …'.

Backtracking to Schliemann's early childhood, Baumann then trots out the most appealing of the archaeologist's autobiographical fables, in which at the tender age of 7 he was shown a picture of Troy in a children's book and promised his father that one day he would go and find the walls of the legendary city. In 1872, in his fiftieth year, Baumann's Schliemann was then spectacularly vindicated, when he identified the site of the city and declared to the world that the walls of Troy were visible once again, bearing the marks of the mighty conflagration inflicted by Agamemnon and his troops. The following year he dug up the treasure of the Trojan king Priam and crowned his beautiful Greek wife with a 3000-year-old golden diadem, hailing her as 'Helen!' The photo of Sophia Schliemann in this unflattering headgear stands with the Mask of Agamemnon as one of the canonical images of mythical archaeology.

This heroic version of Schliemann has always existed alongside a more critical biographical tradition. Lately the archaeologist seems to have really met his nemesis in the form of two American academics, William Calder III and David Traill, who have mounted a systematic campaign to topple Schliemann from the lofty perch he so carefully constructed for himself in his lifetime and expose him as a charlatan and a liar. Using their philological and linguistic skills, the pair have combed through the archive, checking Schliemann's diaries and letters against his published works, meticulously documenting every inconsistency. Almost every high point of the popular Schliemann fable has turned out to be false in some way – perhaps worst of all, the childhood scene with his father seems to have been a self-aggrandising invention of his late middle age. Even biographers who start out *liking* their subjects can end up mired in a sort of literary version of dull marital hatred. For David Traill, who embarked on his study of Schliemann already unenamoured, the whole experience seems to have left him consumed with sharp loathing, some of which found expression in an article in which he methodically compared examples of Schliemann's worst behaviour with the symptoms of psychopathy.

David Traill's animus, however, has also resulted in a book-length biography of Schliemann unmarred by excursions into retrospective diagnosis. Here the archaeologist emerges as a far more interesting character than either the psychopath or the saint – a man of ferocious determination and extraordinary gifts, whose ruthless business instincts often trumped his scholarly integrity and who was never above massaging his discoveries and exaggerating his results for the sake of fame and money. The story of his insatiable hunger for success, his bizarre archaeological good fortune and his grandiose self-advertising has a sort of epic amorality far truer to Homer than the sugar-coated hero of Baumann's overheated imagination. He was a hero for the age of Wagner and Nietzsche, a pagan industrialist, a colossal braggart, a self-made superman. The discovery of the Tomb of Agamemnon by this latter-day Lord of Men reinvented pre-Christian heroism for a post-Christian age.

Heinrich Schliemann was born in 1822 in a remote part of north-eastern Germany near the border with Poland. His father, Ernst, was a Lutheran minister, and in 1823 the family moved to the village of Ankershagen where he took up the post of pastor. Bad tempered, egotistical and promiscuous, Ernst Schliemann was not well suited to the spiritual life. In 1829 he hired an attractive young woman ostensibly to act as a personal maid for his wife Louise. It soon became obvious to the other servants that the girl was his mistress and the affair became common knowledge in the village. After his wife died, his parishioners finally rebelled. Two hundred of them gathered in front of the house to subject him to a little 'rough music', banging pots and pans and throwing things at the windows, a performance that was repeated every Sunday for a month. Their offspring were forbidden to play with the Schliemann children. It may be this humiliating experience, coming so close on the heels of the death of his mother, that accounts for the lonely ferocity of Heinrich's later ambition.

Following his father's suspension without pay from his job, Heinrich was enrolled in a school which did not prepare its pupils for higher education. At the age of 14 he was apprenticed to a grocer in Fürstenberg. Five years of unremitting drudgery were finally brought to an end when he burst a blood vessel moving a heavy cask and was dismissed. He then used a small bequest from his mother to finance his training in book-keeping. In 1841 at the age of 19 he embarked from Hamburg on a ship bound for South America. Only a few days into the voyage, however, the vessel encountered a severe storm and ran aground just off the coast of Holland. Completely destitute, but now, as a result of his brush with death, possessed of a fierce will to live, Schliemann managed to survive on the kindness of strangers until he was able to obtain a position as an office boy at one of the big trading firms in Amsterdam.

Realising that the most invaluable skill he could acquire would be a knowledge of languages, Schliemann then embarked on the tireless intellectual labour that would result in his eventually being fluent in no fewer than fifteen tongues. First he learned English, French and Dutch, and on the strength of these obtained a post as a correspondent and book-keeper with one of the big trading houses. Observing that, although the firm did a lot of business with Russia, no one was conversant with the language, he set himself the task of mastering it, and in six weeks he wrote his first letter to one of the trading partners in Russia. The firm's bosses soon sent him to St Petersburg to act as their agent, and there he set up on his own, embarking on his career as a merchant by dealing in indigo.

Schliemann's linguistic abilities enabled him to become a global player. In California he bought gold dust from the miners to sell on to the Rothschild agent in San Francisco, but left abruptly under suspicion of short-weighting consignments of gold. During the Crimean War he doubled his fortune in a single year by trading in saltpetre, brimstone and metals. This period of his life was marked by extraordinary restlessness; he travelled all over Europe, writing diaries in the language of whatever place he found himself; he spent three months in Egypt where he learned Arabic, and then toured India, China and Japan. His first book, written in French, was an account of his travels in Asia. On one of his trips back to St Petersburg he married the daughter of a friend. The marriage produced three children but was none the less a loveless disaster: Katerina despised her merchant husband

and refused to follow him when he left Russia. After investing a large proportion of his money in property in Paris, he invited his recalcitrant wife to join him in France, but she once again refused, prompting Schliemann to initiate divorce proceedings.

In the late 1860s, unable to return to St Petersburg because of a legal scandal, he settled in Paris, enrolling in classes in philosophy, philology and ancient literature at the Sorbonne. In the summer of 1868, armed with the John Murray *Handbook of Rome and its Environs*, he became a ferociously diligent Grand Tourist, visiting and making notes on every church, museum, site, gallery and monument recommended in the guide. Rome in the 1860s was everywhere pocked with excavations, and he noted in passing that the diggers were uncovering things of great value. Moving on to Naples his interest in archaeology seemed to sharpen, and in his diary he recorded with approval that the pace of the Pompeii excavation had accelerated with the introduction of a railway line to take away the soil.

In July 1868 Schliemann finally found himself in the landscape of Homer. Again, the John Murray *Handbook for Travellers to Greece* seems to have been the inspiration for his itinerary, which now took a distinctly Homeric turn. The section on Ithaca in the *Handbook*, for example, contains a very detailed discussion of the likely location of various places associated with Odysseus, and Schliemann spent a happy few days scrambling around the peaks of the island, following the lead of his guidebook. Schliemann crowned this adventure by taking a spade to the highest point of the peak thought to be the location of Odysseus' palace, and digging up some vases filled with human ashes, about which he asserted with the ridiculous confidence that would become his trademark: 'it is very possible that I have in my five little vases the bodies of Ulysses [the Roman name for Odysseus] and Penelope [his faithful wife]'.

Back in Athens, Schliemann had the encounter that was to determine the course of the rest of his life. Here he met Ernst Ziller, a German architect who had participated in the first attempts to establish the location of ancient Troy using the methods of archaeology. Ziller told him that he had excavated on the acropolis above the village of Bunarbashi, on the west coast of Turkey, at that time the most widely supported contender for the site of the legendary city. Such was Schliemann's enthusiasm for this enterprise that he immediately changed his travel plans and resolved to check out the Trojan Plain for himself. While he waited for the steamer that would take him from the Piraeus to Turkey, he made a quick tour of the Argolid (the ancient name for the lands of Agamemnon's dominion), visiting Mycenae, where he spent the day examining the Lion Gate, the Treasury of Atreus and other famous features of the site.

Once Schliemann reached Turkey he hired some workmen and had them dig a number of trenches at Bunarbashi. They found nothing of interest and he concluded that Troy was not to be sought here. A few days later he met a man called Frank Calvert, an adherent of the theory that Troy was located near the remains of the Hellenistic city of Ilium Novum, or New Troy, a few kilometres north of Bunarbashi. Calvert had made some preliminary investigations at the mound of Hisarlik, the most likely nearby spot for ancient deposits, and had even purchased a part of the site. Realising that Schliemann had the money, the enthusiasm and the drive to finish what he had started, Calvert shared with the merchant all his findings. Schliemann was convinced by his arguments, and resolved to return the following spring to excavate.

Schliemann returned to Paris and immediately threw himself into the task of writing up his Homeric travels into a book. *Ithaque, le Péloponnèse et Troie* was published early in 1869, and with it he earned a doctorate from the University of Rostock. Meanwhile he had set his heart on remarriage, and wrote to a friend in Athens asking him to find a pliant Greek girl to make his wife. From among the photographs he was sent he selected a beautiful schoolgirl, Sophia Engastromenos, thirty years his junior. The union was blessed by her parents, undoubtedly because of Schliemann's wealth, and in September 1869 they were married. After a shaky start, this unlikely and unequal relationship turned into a successful partnership. Sophia, it emerged, possessed just the right combination of loyalty, educability and stubbornness to command the respect of her domineering husband.

In April 1870, impatient with the delays over the matter of a permit to dig, Schliemann travelled to western Turkey and pitched up at Hisarlik, the spot that Calvert had shown him as probably concealing the remains of Troy, where he began, without the permission of the owners of the western half of the mound, to excavate. The results were disappointing, but there was enough to persuade him to return the following year to embark on the legal excavation of the site. Unfortunately, the beginning of the second season was even more disappointing than the first. The top stratum of the mound was clearly Hellenistic in date (after 325 BC) and therefore far too late to represent the city of the Trojan War. Directly below that seemed to be the remains of a Stone Age settlement, a level far too early to have anything to do with Homer. Since the Homeric heroes wielded bronze weapons, the Troy of legend would have to be sought in the Bronze Age. The problem – which Schliemann never fully recognised – was that the builders of the Hellenistic city had levelled the mound, shaving off a whole millennium of deposits. Traces of the Bronze Age thus appeared only where the strata curved downwards at the edges of the mound. This meant that as Schliemann dug *deeper* more and more objects of bronze and copper appeared, convincing him that the Homeric city lay at the lowest level of the deposits.

The following year, in an act of archaeological vandalism egregious even by the standards of the day, Schliemann ploughed an enormous trench, 79 metres wide and 14 metres deep, right through the middle of the north–south axis of the mound, shifting in the process some 78,000 cubic metres of earth. Ironically, he thus destroyed much of the level now considered to correspond to the date of the Trojan War, instructing the workmen to dismantle any buildings that obstructed their progress towards bedrock. In a passage calculated to bring a tear to an archaeologist's eye, he complains that the workmen would leave their labours to watch as their colleagues sent the huge stones hurtling off down the sides of the mound. Although in private he was haunted by doubt as to the identification of the first, and then the second level of deposits with Homeric Troy – confiding in one correspondent that the citadel was depressingly small, not much bigger than Trafalgar Square – in public he stuck to his story, identifying various structures with landmarks from the *Iliad* such as the 'Great Tower of Ilium', 'Priam's Palace' and the 'Scaean Gate'.

In 1873 Schliemann dug up the treasure that would make him a household name. In *Troy and Its Remains* he tells how, spying a glint of gold among the ruins of the city walls, he dismissed the workers for an early breakfast and cut into the mud with his own knife, pulling out an enormous hoard of jewellery and other gold items and loading them into the skirt of his indefatigable wife Sophia (who was actually in Athens at the time).

By fudging the findspot, and conflating a few separate discoveries, Schliemann turned the discovery of 'Priam's treasure' into a lurid bit of Homeric detective work, reconstructing from some fragments of wood and a copper key the hasty exodus of 'some member of Priam's family' from the citadel, clutching to his or her bosom a box full of treasure. On 5 August 1873, an account of the discovery of the hoard was published in the German newspaper *Augsburger Allgemeine Zeitung*, causing an immediate sensation, with abbreviated versions appearing all over the world. Even for those people who did not accept the identification of the treasure with King Priam, the sheer quantity of gold was amazing.

After finding Troy, the next challenge was to locate the Tomb of Agamemnon. In 1874, sure that he would be denied a permit by the Greek government, Schliemann made his first unauthorised excavations at Mycenae. These were halted by the local authorities. Finally, in 1876, after making some lavish contributions to the Greek Archaeological Society, he was put in charge of the Society's excavations at Mycenae on the condition that he undertake the work at his own expense. Panagiotis Stamatakis, a young Greek archaeologist, was appointed to supervise the excavations on behalf of the Greek government. Schliemann and Stamatakis squabbled incessantly. The conscientious young Greek was appalled by Schliemann's high-handed methods, his single-minded disregard of all but Bronze Age remains and his attachment to an industrial scale of digging that made the job of close supervision impossible. Despite these difficulties and tensions, the excavations bore spectacular fruit (illustration 10).

In his first book of Homeric topography, *Ithaque, le Péloponnèse et Troie*, Schliemann had advanced his own interpretation of the Mycenae tour in Pausanias' guidebook. 'Clytemnestra and Aegisthus', Pausanias declares, 'were buried at a little distance from the wall; for they were deemed unworthy to be buried within the walls, where Agamemnon himself and those who had been murdered with him were laid.' A few later commentators had assumed that the walls Pausanias referred to were the slight and fragmentary remains of the wall around the lower city. Schliemann represented himself as defying all received wisdom when he decided that Pausanias could only mean the massive walls encircling the citadel itself, although in fact about half of the earlier nineteenth-century visitors to the site came to same conclusion. Accordingly, when his workmen unearthed a circle of stone slabs at a spot inside the citadel just to the right of the Lion Gate, and found within it a series of individual upright stones, some with elaborate relief sculptures, he announced that these were the tombstones of 'the sepulchres which Pausanias, following the tradition, attributes to Atreus, to the "king of men" Agamemnon, to his charioteer Eurymedon, to Cassandra, and to their companions'. As his workmen excavated beneath the first of the tombstones, a grave was revealed, hewn out of the rock, with deep, square sides. At first the finds comprised a confusing mass of seemingly random artefacts: bone

10. The frieze on the north side of Schliemann's tomb depicting him and his wife directing an excavation. Schliemann, in the classic imperial garb of pith hat and long double-breasted jacket, commands his Greek and Turkish workers with a gesture reminiscent of King Proteus supervising the building of Tiryns on the first frieze in the series.

buttons covered in gold, human bones, pig bones, fragments of vases. Eventually, however, the deep shaft graves beneath the tombstones would yield a treasure so stunning that his account of its finding still astonishes.

On 13 November 1876, towards the evening, came the first indication of the riches to come. Having been forced by heavy rain to abandon the excavation of the first tomb, the workmen found within the shallower second grave a partially burned corpse covered in funerary jewellery made of thin sheets of gold. The following day, in the same shaft, they encountered a layer of pebbles, below which they found the remains of two more bodies. All three corpses in this grave turned out to be covered in the same gold ornaments: five diadems of thin gold plate piped with copper wire and covered in repoussé work. In addition two of the bodies sported a series of five flimsy gold crosses formed of four oval leaves joined at the centre. Also in the grave were obsidian knives, terracotta vases, a silver cup and a mass of little terracotta figurines.

On 23 November Schliemann reached the bedrock of the third shaft grave. Here he found the 'bones of three women … covered with masses of gold'. These funeral ornaments take no fewer than forty-six pages of Schliemann's final excavation report to describe. Among the artefacts decorating the corpses were several large gold diadems; 701 round plates of gold covered in repoussé work of spirals, cuttlefish, butterflies, stars, leaves and flowers; gold ornaments in the shape of griffins, lions and stags; and a gold brooch with a silver pin in the form of a woman or a goddess with outstretched arms under a sprouting pattern of leaves. Accompanying the bodies were two pairs of ornamental scales; some mysterious objects in agate and crystal and silver; a gold goblet, a gold box and various other gold vessels; sceptres of gold, silver and crystal; amber jewellery; and seals of gold, agate, sardonyx and amethyst. Alongside the bones of the women were the gold funeral shrouds of two babies.

The next tomb to which he turned was similarly rich. Here the five bodies – thought by Schliemann to all be male – were 'literally smothered in jewels', accompanied by the same gold discs and funerary diadems, plus a massive and unusually solid armlet made of two sheets of gold sandwiching a sheet of silver. Forty-six swords were found in this grave, including two inlaid daggers of exquisite workmanship, one with running lions and the other depicting a lion hunt. It also contained a large number of fine gold and silver vessels, mostly goblets of various forms. Among these was a gold cup that was greeted with particular excitement by Schliemann as answering to the description in the eleventh book of the *Iliad* of a cup brought to Troy by Agamemnon's advisor, King Nestor.

Three of the five bodies in this tomb were adorned with gold masks, which Schliemann claimed represented individual portraits of the dead men whose faces they covered. The first, he suggested, had a large, oval, youthful face with a small, thin-lipped mouth; the second had round cheeks, full lips and a low forehead; the third 'exhibits again a totally different physiognomy: the wrinkles to the right and left above the mouth, and the expression of the very large mouth with thin lips, can leave no doubt that we have here the portrait of a man of more advanced age'. (This was entirely wishful thinking on his part, as the masks are extremely crude and stylised.) The fifth grave was, by the standards of the tombs already opened, a modest find: one burial, equipped for the afterlife with a golden goblet, some swords, knives and vases.

Finally, Schliemann returned to the first sepulchre, which had dried out during the weeks of fine weather. Three bodies lay at the bottom of the shaft, three men, Schliemann declared, of truly heroic proportions, to judge from the size of the thigh bones. They were accompanied by another dazzling hoard including gold breastplates, bronze swords, an alabaster vase and a drinking cup of the same material, and twelve rectangular plates of gold inscribed with elaborate scenes, eventually identified as the sides of a wooden box. The first of the corpses, lying in the south end of the tomb, was wearing the gold mask now famous as the Mask of Agamemnon. When the mask was removed, the skull immediately crumbled away to dust and only a few bones could be saved, including those of the legs. The second body had been moved in antiquity, had no mask, and was almost completely decomposed. But the third body, lying in the north, wore a heavy gold mask, underneath which 'the round face, with all its flesh, had been wonderfully preserved'. Although there was no vestige of hair, both eyes were perfectly visible, and the mouth, forced open by the weight bearing down on it, was wide open, displaying 'thirty-two beautiful teeth'.

It was this body, the one whose flesh was preserved, that sent Schliemann into real Homeric raptures. In a telegram to a Greek newspaper he said: 'This corpse very much resembles the image which my imagination formed long ago of wide-ruling Agamemnon', later abbreviated to the apocryphal but catchy, 'Today I gazed upon the face of Agamemnon'. News of the discovery spread rapidly, and people poured into Mycenae in their thousands to view the corpse. Doctors examined the 'beautiful teeth' and pronounced the man to have been about 35 when he died. A pharmacist was requisitioned from the nearby town of Nauplion, who poured gum arabic over the body to harden it. A small trench was dug all round the corpse and a horizontal incision was cut right into the soft rock, forming a two-inch slab on which the body was lifted clear of the tomb and carried, on the shoulders of a willing group of men, to the nearby village, to be forwarded to Athens as soon as a suitable resting place was arranged.

If Schliemann had indeed imagined Agamemnon to look like the body in the north end of the first shaft grave, it was a thoroughly perverse image of an ancient hero. There are two illustrations in *Mycenae* from which we might get an idea of what this creature looked like. The first is an engraving taken from an oil painting that Schliemann commissioned at the time. This is an almost indecipherable depiction of the skull and ribs of what looks like a skeleton, except that there are round, closed eyelids where the eye sockets would be. The eyes, sitting oddly far apart and low in the face, give a foetal effect to the features, and the overall impression is of a sort of deformed pathos. The other illustration comprises an engraving of the gold death mask that covered the head of this corpse. Schliemann is moved to apologise for the state of this portrait of Agamemnon, explaining away his disappointing appearance as a product of the crushed condition in which the mask was found. This clean-shaven, fat, round face with cramped little features bunched up in the middle evokes podgy executive more than Homeric warlord, and Schliemann does not linger over his description. Instead he moves right along to the dashing moustachioed figure cut by the golden mask now associated with Agamemnon, drooling over his 'altogether Hellenic' features, 'the long thin nose, running in a direct line with the forehead' and the 'well-proportioned lips'. He also draws attention to the beard and upward-pointing moustache, an arrangement of facial hair so modish that he wryly comments 'there is nothing new under the sun'. This mask was the very image of a fashionable European prince of Schliemann's time and, by virtue of appearing as the illustration to every account of the discovery, effortlessly usurped the role of Agamemnon from its uncharismatic sibling (illustration 11).

Having found his Agamemnon and excavated the richest Bronze Age burials ever discovered, Schliemann quit Mycenae and returned to Athens to prepare his report and get ready for the hectic lecture circuit that his fame now demanded. His leaving Mycenae was, to say the least, premature, and it was left to the long-suffering Stamatakis to excavate another two shafts, one outside the Grave Circle, containing another fabulous array of gold but no bodies, and a sixth tomb, this one inside the Grave Circle and containing bronze and gold grave goods and two skeletons.

Schliemann's excavation report, *Mycenae: a narrative of researches and discoveries at Mycenae and Tiryns*, takes the form of a day-to-day journal, and is confusing in places, with too little information to indicate where important finds were made, and many internal contradictions. But the spectacular finds were illustrated with beautiful engravings, and the sheer quantity of precious artefacts combined with the strangeness and sophistication of their artistry put even Priam's treasure in the shade. *Mycenae* was the triumph that sealed Schliemann's fame, and even critics of the unsoundness of the merchant's methods had to acknowledge the scale of his successes.

11. The gold death mask worn by the well-preserved corpse from the first shaft grave. This is the face that should by rights have claimed the title of the Mask of Agamemnon but it was quickly usurped by the more distinguished features of the handsome bearded mask found in the same tomb.

Chapter X of the book discussed the burning question of the identity of the five tombs with the burial places of Agamemnon and his companions. The argument pivots on Schliemann's conviction – continually buttressed by his narrative presentation of the finds – that the bodies in each tomb were burned and buried at the same time. So patently false was this contention that Wilhelm Dörpfeld, the brilliant young architect who became Schliemann's principal assistant in 1882, was able to confound it just by studying Schliemann's own testimony. From Schliemann's diary, for example, it is clear that he first found one body in the second grave and then two others at a deeper level. In the book, by contrast, he narrates that he found them all together, at the same depth. For the less critically inclined reader of *Mycenae*, however, the assertion that 'all the twelve men, three women, and perhaps two or three children, had been murdered simultaneously and burned at the same time' would have sealed the case. How else to explain this extraordinary combination of wickedness and splendour – the murder of the inhabitants of the graves and their burial with such honour – except by recourse to the story of Agamemnon's terrible fate? Gone for ever were the days when the sight of Mycenae would produce the standardised response of the Enlightenment antiquarian; Agamemnon was now flesh and blood, a legend resurrected, an ancient hero awakened to fight the wars of modernity.

SAVIOUR OR ANTICHRIST?

On Monday 18 December 1876 *The Times* of London carried an anonymous leader on its front page about the finding of Agamemnon's tomb. 'Antiquity', it ringingly announced, '… has suddenly made a splendid revelation'. The editorial is a splendidly overwrought bit of journalistic excess, presenting Schliemann's dig as the fulfilment of a destiny that had been unfolding since the darkest recesses of antiquity. A potted history of Mycenae, recounted with more brio than accuracy, portrays the city as cursed, a place that 'emerged into a flash of glory' only to be 'instantly quenched in crimes and catastrophe'. The article then suggests that the terrible legend of the House of Atreus had cast its malign spell over the whole Peloponnese, repelling civilised travellers and sending only 'Greeks, barbarians, Turks and Albanians' to the ruins of Mycenae, to throw 'everything about in the wildest confusion' (note the inclusion of Greeks in this list …). No mention is made of Edward Dodwell, Lord Elgin or the Marquis of Sligo, but Robert Chandler, the one English Dilettante who managed to get lost on the way to the ruins, is quoted verbatim. All this leads irresistibly to the conclusion that:

> … *some misleading genie like the instinct ascribed to certain birds, had all these ages been baffling the curiosity of prying*

visitors, by distracting their attention and putting them on one
false scout or another, till in fullness of time the great KING of
MEN who found a bard in HOMER should have his royal state
once more shown to the world by Dr SCHLIEMANN.

After making a patriotic aside about the percentage of
'British tin' found in the bronze of Mycenae, the author of
the leader then boldly apportions the gold jewellery from the
third shaft grave among the leading ladies of the Agamemnon
story. 'Have we indeed the whole jewel-box and toilet of the
ill-fated prophetess who told everybody his doom and her own
in vain, and who suffered the additional misery of foreknow-
ing all the misery to come?' he asks, immediately replying in
the affirmative: 'CASSANDRA is here – a fairy-like form,
with all her pretty trinkets, her earrings, necklaces, bracelets,
hairpins, lockets and clasps.' In a completely novel interpretation he then identifies one of the other female burials from
the same grave: 'It was CLYTEMNESTRA that buried them
with her,' he declares, 'soon to follow her to the same tomb.'
Eventually he reaches the climax of Schliemann's discoveries:
'Strangest of all, the hero himself, AGAMEMNON, remains,
and is found to be just such a giant as a hundred Chiefs would
choose for their leader – a head and shoulders taller than all.'

It is only in the last paragraph that we finally learn the
purpose of all this portentous rhetoric. 'But why was this discovery reserved for the latter end of the nineteenth century?'
the author demands, before trumpeting that Agamemnon's
awakening has come right in the 'nick of time', prefiguring
the arrival of a great political and military leader: 'What is it
that all Europe is looking for? It is the KING of MEN, the
great head of the Hellenic race …'.

Schliemann's archaeological feat turns out to be intimately bound up with another leader on the same front page, this one a long rant about the folly and wickedness of the British government's handling of the 'Eastern Question'. Disraeli's conservative administration, much to the disgust of *The Times*, was committed to a policy of appeasing and propping up the tattered remnants of the Ottoman empire as a bulwark against the expansion of Russia in central Asia and eastern Europe. In April 1876 the Sublime Porte – the Ottoman central government – had responded to a feeble attempted uprising in Bulgaria with incredible ferocity. Over the summer, just as Schliemann began his excavation of Mycenae, the news had reached Britain of thousands of slaughtered Bulgarian Christians, whipping up a gigantic political storm. Now Disraeli's secretary of state for India was on his way to Constantinople to meet the Russian ambassador, and *The Times* was railing against the government's refusal to support Russia's crusade against the Ottomans. Poor old Agamemnon had emerged from the soil of a remote corner of the Peloponnese to find himself embroiled in yet another updated version of the Trojan War, his reappearance hailed by *The Times* as a fitting model for 'the man to head the entire Greek race and the races mixed with it in their impending struggle with the remnants of the Asiatic power'.

This modern Agamemnon would be 'a true Philhellene, a scholar, a statesman, and man of unflinching courage and irrepressible enterprise, full of resources and ready to look in the face a rival or a foe'. It went without saying that the hero who took on the mantle of the struggle against the Turks, as defined by English liberal anti-Ottoman sentiment of the 1870s, would also be Christian. Greek was not only the tongue of Homer and Aeschylus, but also the language in which the New Testament was written. In the centuries since Pausanias visited Mycenae, the lands of Agamemnon and those of Priam had taken on the great divide of Christian versus Muslim. When Schliemann first fell in love with the shaft-grave corpse's thirty-two beautiful teeth and dubbed it 'Agamemnon', he brought into being an icon of Christendom, a king of men who would, in the course of the next half century, be progressively Aryanised, paganised and secularised, a saviour who would mutate briefly into the Antichrist in preparation for his final emergence as a fascist *Führer*.

On 22 March 1877 Schliemann arrived in London and that evening gave the first of a series of hugely successful talks on his excavation of Mycenae. The archaeologist was rapturously received everywhere that he appeared: he was appointed to honorary membership of the British Archaeological Association, the Royal Archaeological Institute, the Royal Institute of British Architects and the Royal Historical Society. In a poignant celebration of his humble origins he was made the honoured guest at a banquet of the Grocers' and Salters' companies where he spoke of his teenage experiences as an apprentice grocer. London was the most welcoming of the European cities which Schliemann visited on his lecture tour, and he declared to a friend that he was writing his book on Mycenae in English because it was in England that he was 'respected and loved'. The English, long considered the practical, unimaginative industrialists of Europe, turned out to lead the world in their inexhaustible appetite for Schliemann's brand of modern myth-making.

Schliemann's first London talk on Mycenae was addressed to a crowded meeting of the Society of Antiquaries attended by the erstwhile and future prime minister, William Ewart Gladstone (illustration 12). Gladstone, possibly the author of the *Times* leader, was the absolute embodiment of the English love affair with Schliemann's Agamemnon, his championing of the archaeologist's wilder interpretations marching in lockstep with his passionately philhellenic attitude to the Eastern Question. After his 1875 resignation as leader of the Liberal Party he had burst back into the forefront of British politics with an incendiary pamphlet on the Ottoman massacres in Bulgaria: 'There is not a cannibal in the South Sea Islands, whose indignation would not arise and overboil at the recital of that which has been done ...' etc. (As one rather more impartial British observer, Edith Durham, noted in 1905: 'When a Muslim kills a Muslim it does not count; when a Christian kills a Muslim it is a righteous act; when a Christian kills a Christian it is an error of judgment better not talked about; it is only when a Muslim kills a Christian that we arrive at full-blown atrocity.')

Gladstone was also a prolific Homeric scholar, finding time during his meteoric parliamentary career to produce the nineteenth century's single most extensive (and eccentric) body of Homeric commentary. Long before Schliemann's excavations he had regarded Homer's poems as realist history, and had devoted much of his spare time to a quixotic effort to reconcile the epics of his beloved pagan bard with Christian Scripture. In 1858 he made his classical debut with a hastily written and somewhat-ridiculed three volumes on the spiritual parallels between the *Iliad* and the Book of Genesis, a conviction he cleaved to his whole life.

By dint of persistent badgering, Schliemann eventually succeeded in the greatest social coup of his career,

12. Schliemann speaking to the Society of Antiquaries in London on 22 March 1877. The figure seated in the chair in the foreground may represent Gladstone, who was present at the meeting.

managing to persuade Gladstone to contribute a preface to his volume on the Mycenaean excavations. The archaeologist had chosen his spokesman well. Great Britain's most famous politician turned out to be a Homeric literalist who outstripped Schliemann himself in his imaginative powers and his tendentious reconstructions. First he recaps the account of Agamemnon's assassination as told in the *Odyssey*, picking out the detail that Clytemnestra did not 'vouchsafe to her husband the last office of mercy and compassion, by closing his mouth and eyes in death'. Referring the reader to Schliemann's weird engraving of the mummified body from the first tomb, Gladstone then wonderingly asserts that 'Dr. Schliemann assures that the right eye, which alone could be seen with tolerable clearness, was not entirely shut … while the teeth of the upper jawbone … did not quite join those of the lower.' Here he goes beyond Schliemann himself in his desire to read on the ancient remains the actual marks of the story, down to the minutiae of the Homeric account. The mummified body is assumed to be that of Agamemnon, and to retain on its bizarre features the impress of his tragic fate (illustration 13).

To account for the fact that the bodies were not just then thrown out of the city for the dogs and vultures, but buried with honour, covered in the weight in gold of nearly 'five thousand British sovereigns', Gladstone indulges in a superb piece of Schliemannesque reconstruction. First Aegisthus and Clytemnestra, to appease that constituency of their subjects who might harbour some loyalty to the murdered king, buried their victims within the walls of the citadel in deep graves. But the graves made were a little too small for these supermen and the bodies were crammed in, because 'honour

13. This bizarre image depicts the well-preserved corpse in the first shaft grave, complete with the 'thirty-two beautiful teeth' swooned over by Schliemann. It was in these distorted features that the archaeologist purported to recognise the face of Agamemnon. Gladstone went a step further and insisted that the face bore out the details of the legend of Agamemnon's murder.

stopped with the preparation of the tomb, and the rest, less visible to the public eye, was left to spite or haste'. Then it was left to Orestes, when he returned to avenge his father, to make reparations for the manner of their interment by opening the tombs and covering the bodies in gold 'to replace in the wasted bodies the seemliness and majesty of nature ....'.

Even more than in Schliemann's work, there is in Gladstone's preface an absurd contrast between the loving narrative detail of the reconstruction and the muteness of the actual artefacts. Perhaps the hero's resurrection was too politically useful in the politician's crusade against the Ottomans to allow for doubt or reason.

Gladstone was not alone in his attempts to reconcile Homer and Scripture. The Christianising of the Homeric heroes turned out to be an all-purpose ideological tool, as useful against Jews as against Muslims. One of Schliemann's closest associates was the director of the French School at Athens, Emile Burnouf, a rabid anti-Semite whose anthropological work was dedicated to proving that Christianity had an Aryan rather than a Semitic origin. Excited by the fact that the ruins of Troy were full of artefacts featuring his favourite symbol, Burnouf wrote to Schliemann in 1872 exhorting him that 'the Swastika should be regarded as a sign of the Aryan race'. 'It should also be noted,' he continued 'that the Jews have completely rejected it.' Schliemann obediently fell in with Burnouf's agenda, announcing in *Troy and Its Remains* that 'This winter I have read in Athens many excellent works of celebrated scholars on Indian antiquities … and I now perceive that these crosses upon the Trojan terracottas are of the highest importance to archaeology.'

Aryan theory was first launched by linguists who noted the similarities between Sanskrit, Persian, Greek and other European languages and proposed that the 'Aryas' of the Hindu epic the Rig-Veda were a fair-haired, light-skinned people who had invaded India from their central Asian base, fanning out thereafter into Persia and finally Europe.

Schliemann, eager as always to join the scholarly in-crowd, contributed his own particular insight to the Aryanist project, boasting that he alone had 'recognised at first glance' the same swastika symbol found at Troy on some prehistoric pots dug up in Germany. While these symbols had 'given rise to very many learned discussions', he noted complacently, no one else had 'recognised the mark as that exceedingly significant religious symbol of our remote ancestors'. (The sobriety of such acts of recognition may be judged by the juxtaposition on one page of *Troy and Its Remains* of Schliemann's 'proof' that the 'primitive Trojans ... belonged to the Aryan race' with his bizarre claim that the two large toads that hopped out of the lower reaches of the excavation 'must have spent 3000 years in these depths'. 'It is very interesting', mused the archaeologist, 'to find in the ruins of Troy living creatures from the time of Hector and Andromache, even though these creatures are but toads.')

A couple of years after the publication of *Troy and Its Remains*, Burnouf hit the presses with his book *The Science of Religions*. In this tract Burnouf derived the Christian cross from the swastika. He declared that the symbol represented the two pieces of wood which were laid cross-wise upon one another before the sacrificial altars of the Aryans, and then rubbed together in order to produce the holy fire. In one of the tortuous chains of reasoning typical of this genre of mytho-anthropology, he then linked the swastika with the Vedic fire god Agni, and by extension to Prometheus, whose torment he understood as a prefiguration of the crucifixion of Christ: 'When Jesus was put to death by the Jews, this old Aryan symbol was easily applied to him.' 'Christian archaeology' was only one arrow in Burnouf's sinister quiver. Most of the burden of proof of his theory rested on the shoulders of a doctrine which held that the 'white races' alone were capable of higher thought and that the Jewish brain stopped developing after the age of 'fifteen or sixteen'.

Having burdened the swastika symbol with such cultural, religious and racial significance in *Troy and Its Remains*, it was incumbent on Schliemann to find the symbol repeated at Mycenae, but its occurrence turned out to be disappointingly infrequent. He did his best with what he had, asserting in *Mycenae* that the swastika 'may often be seen' on the painted pottery but failing to illustrate any examples. Similarly, he described but did not illustrate a terracotta disc covered in swastikas, 'the sign which occurs so frequently in the ruins of Troy'. Straining desperately after the same connection, he later suggested that a completely dissimilar curly six-pointed ornament on some of the gold discs in the third shaft grave was 'derived' from the swastika: 'the artist has only added two more arms and curved all of them'.

Despite the difficulties with linking the symbolism of Troy and Mycenae, the common Aryan roots of the two peoples became something of a truism. Emile Burnouf contributed a section to *Mycenae* that situated Agamemnon and his unfortunate ancestors as one of the 'prehistoric dynasties of the Aryan races'. When Schliemann came to publish his final statement on Troy, his *Troja* of 1884, it opened with a preface by the Professor of Assyriology at Oxford, A. H. Sayce, who trumpeted that 'we, as well as the Greeks of the age of Agamemnon, can hail the subjects of Priam as brethren in blood and speech'. *Troja* was also adorned with an appendix by the Anglo-German journalist Karl Blind asserting the 'Teutonic kinship of Trojans and Thrakians', whose first sentence ringingly declared that 'the Trojans were originally a Teutonic tribe'. In 1889 a Polish librarian named Michael Zmigrodski, inspired by Schliemann's spindle whorls, hosted a display at the Paris Exposition that brought together drawings of over 300 objects with swastikas on them, celebrating the symbol as the heraldic device of the Aryo-Germanic family. Zmigrodski was an anti-Semite whose aim was to prove that 'in a very ancient epoch, our Indo-European ancestors professed social and religious ideas more noble and elevated than those of other races'.

Only a few years after Schliemann's last word on Troy appeared, the one-time classics professor Friedrich Nietzsche published the most provocative and influential interpretation of the newly 'Aryanised' Homeric heroes. Nietzsche's celebration of early Greek 'master morality' in his 1887 *On the Genealogy of Morality* demonstrates the extent to which Schliemann's arguments were by now part of the taken-for-granted background to any discussion of the Homeric epics. Throughout the text Nietzsche assumes the historical reality of the Homeric heroes and insists on their Aryan roots. At one point he even chastises Schliemann's closest collaborator, the famous German pathologist and anthropologist Rudolf Virchow, for suggesting that the Celts were dark haired. The philosopher's portrait of the splendid bestiality of the Mycenaean aristocrats is constantly run together with reflec-

tions on German ancestry, a set of connections that culmi-
nates in this infamous flight of historical fancy:

> *At the centre of all these noble races we cannot fail to see the
> blond beast of prey, the magnificent* blond beast *avidly prowl-
> ing round for spoil and victory; this hidden centre needs release
> from time to time, the beast must out again, must return to the
> wild: — Roman, Arabian, Germanic, Japanese nobility, Homeric
> heroes, Scandinavian Vikings — in this requirement they are all
> alike ... The deep and icy mistrust which the German arouses
> as soon as he comes to power, which we see again even today
> — is still the aftermath of that inextinguishable horror with
> which Europe viewed the raging of the blond Germanic beast
> for centuries ...*

In 1895 one of the strangest and yet most enduring interpretations of Schliemann's excavations first appeared, penned
by a friend of Gladstone's called Robert Anderson. Anderson
was born in 1841 in Dublin and was saved for Christ by a thrill-
ing sermon that he heard at the age of 19. After studying law
he was called to the Bar and went on to become the British
government's Irish Agent, helping them to investigate and
break the movement against British rule in Ireland. In 1888,
when London was in the grip of the Jack the Ripper scare, he
was appointed assistant commissioner of the Metropolitan
Police.

During this distinguished career, Anderson wrote no
fewer than seventeen major books on biblical themes. While
he was assistant commissioner of the Met he published the
work for which he is now primarily remembered, a volume
of Christian prophecy that would run to ten editions in his

own lifetime, was republished in the 1980s, and is available today on the internet at domains such as 'raptureready.com'. *The Coming Prince* is an exhaustive interpretation of the prophetic vision of the 'seventy weeks' vouchsafed to Daniel by the Angel Gabriel. In the final chapter Anderson details when and where he believes the 'coming prince' – the Antichrist whose appearance heralds the second coming of Christ – will emerge. It turns out that the prophecy may already be in the process of fulfilment. Clearly impressed by the oracular tone of the *Times* leader on the finding of Agamemnon's tomb, Anderson quotes it at length and then intones that 'The realization of this dream [the coming of the modern Agamemnon] will be the fulfilment of prophecy.'

Schliemann's finding of Agamemnon's tomb not only warns Anderson as to the imminence of the coming of the Antichrist, it helps him pinpoint *where* Satan will emerge: 'In connection with this dream or legend of the reappearance of Agamemnon, it is remarkable that the language of Daniel's second vision has led some to fix on Greece as the very place in which the Man of prophecy shall have his rise.' Betraying the same preoccupation with the Eastern Question as his friend William Gladstone, he speculates that the Antichrist will be 'the head of some new Principality to arise in the final dismemberment of Turkey ...'. In the even darker vision of the assistant commissioner, Gladstone's Agamemnon, smiter of Pashas, had mutated into the devil himself.

6

THE BIRTH OF THE BRONZE AGE

It is quite possible that when Pausanias made his tour of Mycenae in the second century AD the myth of the Grave Circle was already in place. If Schliemann was right, the present double circle of slabs right inside the Lion Gate does in fact mark the place that Pausanias' tour guide pointed out as covering the tombs of Agamemnon and his entourage. Schliemann would then stand as the last in a long line, the inheritor of a mangled tradition in which the gold-filled graves of Mycenae's ancient rulers were confused with the burial place of the city's legendary 'king of kings'. One might even go so far as to say that Heinrich Schliemann was not so much the first archaeologist of Bronze Age Greece as the last practitioner of the Cult of the Hero, a Victorian pagan whose self-aggrandising bestowal of Homeric names on anonymous bones served as part of a campaign to secure his own immortality.

But while a larger-than-life cast of politicos, romantics and would-be prophets embraced Agamemnon and lionised Schliemann, back at the site itself mythology was gradually yielding to method. Once Schliemann and Stamatakis had retired from the fray, a German military engineer called Bernard Steffen made the first detailed maps of Mycenae and the surrounding area, revealing the network of Bronze

Age roads radiating out from the city. Shortly afterwards, Christos Tsountas, a young archaeologist from the Greek Archaeological Society, began to excavate at Mycenae, labouring there for eighteen years and producing the first definitive account of the civilisation of the Bronze Age Aegean. Other Bronze Age sites and artefacts – some of which had been uncovered before Schliemann had catapulted the Heroic Age into the headlines – could now be placed in context. In 1890 the German archaeologist Karl Schuchhardt did Schliemann the inestimable service of publishing an updated account of his excavations 'in the light of today's science' (for the site of Mycenae, this amounted to reinterpreting the shaft graves according to the work of Christos Tsountas). As the twentieth century rolled around, archaeologists went to work on the island of Crete, supplying an extraordinary prequel to the story of Mycenae in the form of the even earlier Bronze Age culture of the Minoans. In the 1920s, a team from the British School in Athens scraped patiently away at the remains of Mycenae for three years, returning in 1939 for one more season before the outbreak of war. Although Homer remained the inspiration for the whole enterprise, the dubbing of tombs and other sites with legendary names became less and less literal, with Agamemnon appearing only as a late Mycenaean king whose expensive foreign policy had made him unable to leave his mark on the physical fabric of his city.

Christos Tsountas, the individual who properly deserves the title of Father of the Greek Bronze Age, was a precociously brilliant and prodigiously hard-working young man of 27 when he was entrusted with the further excavation of Mycenae on behalf of the Greek Archaeological Society. Between 1884 and 1902 he excavated over 100 chamber tombs and cleared most of the acropolis, exposing, among other things, the badly eroded remains of a palace at the summit and revealing a hidden passageway on the eastern side that led down to an underground cistern. In 1893 he published *Mycenae and the Mycenaean Civilisation* in Greek, a longer version of which, co-authored with the American classicist J. Irving Mannat, appeared in English in 1897 under the title *The Mycenaean Age: a study of the monuments and culture of pre-Homeric Greece*. This is still one of the most beguiling works about the Mycenaeans, lively without being fanciful, accurate without being dry, and leavened with great wit and charm. Once Tsountas focused his remarkable powers of analysis and his unflagging energy on to the problem, the remains of Mycenae began, at last, to speak for themselves.

The chorus of praise that always accompanies accounts of Tsountas' work sounds only one dissenting note: he did not fully respect the potsherd, that virtually indestructible fragment whose changing styles comprise a stratigraphic calendar of prehistory. Working just before the age in which the potsherd was accorded its full status in his discipline as the diagnostic object par excellence, he committed the grave sin of actually chucking out some of what he found. Quibbling aside, *The Mycenaean Age* was the first work of synthesis that delineated a vision of the Bronze Age Aegean as a whole. Tsountas dismissed the conjectures about Agamemnon and his entourage, arranged the architectural achievements of the Mycenaeans in the correct relative order, assembled the evidence for Mycenaean dress and religious worship and published the first few examples of inscribed artefacts from Mycenae. One of his most important scholarly achievements was the establishment of a chronological framework for Mycenaean civilisation, based on his knowledge of recent excavations in Egypt. Because Egypt was a literate civilisation with a well-developed sense of its own history, Mycenaean objects found there, as well as the Egyptian artefacts that occasionally turned up in prehistoric Greece, allowed the different pottery styles of the Aegean Bronze Age to be correlated with the rise and fall of dated Egyptian dynasties. Tsountas suggested a period from the sixteenth to the twelfth centuries BC for the 'bloom-time' of Mycenaean civilisation – still considered a sound estimate today.

Tsountas' Mycenaeans were, above all, a bellicose lot, who 'looked on war as the only liberal profession' and built their cities accordingly. Mycenae, indeed, seemed to him to be placed 'not for defence but for aggression'. Synthesising literary and archaeological evidence, he suggested that the city was the military outpost of two successive waves of warlike proto-Greek immigrants: the marsh-dwelling Danaans who buried their dead in the shaft graves exhumed by Schliemann and the mountain-dwelling Achaeans who built the great beehive tombs outside the citadel. The Achaeans had descended into Greek myth as the Pelopids, legendary founders of the city and Agamemnon's ancestors. Under them the city rose to its Homeric eminence and became the capital of the Hellenic world. But a mere two generations after the Trojan War another wave of invaders, the Dorians, successfully besieged the Lion Gate and torched Mycenae. The new lords recognised that the key to dominance of the plain was the citadel of Argos and made that their base, while Mycenae became a feeble dependency. For the next thousand years, in spite of a couple of periods of rather half-hearted reoccupation, the remains of Mycenae's splendid Bronze Age architecture would enjoy the protection of the city's political insignificance and historical marginality.

In 1876 Schliemann had uncovered the remains of a house next to the Grave Circle that he identified as the 'probable royal palace' of Mycenae. (With epic hyperbole, he assured his readers that the house was 'vast', and it might have been with some disappointment that they learned that the largest room was '18½ feet long by 13½ feet broad'.) It was left to Tsountas to discover the actual palace on the summit of the acropolis, and to excavate the graceful flight of steps by which the citizens of Mycenae approached their royal family (these are among the only ancient steps on the site; the stairs that snake up the acropolis from the entrance to the citadel are modern). Little more than the badly eroded ground plan of the lower rooms remained, overlaid by the ruins of a later Doric temple from the seventh century BC. With the help of Homer and the better-preserved Bronze Age palace that Schliemann had excavated at Tiryns, Tsountas reconstructed this building for his readers in all its splendid Homeric barbarity, a two-storey warlord's showpiece built around a hearth-cum-throne room, the walls clad in gaudy frescoes and lustrous metals, the flat wooden roof thatched with reeds and plaster.

To Tsountas' obvious delight, the palace at Mycenae seemed to settle one of the livelier disputes about the correspondence between the Homeric poems and what was revealed by the modern spade. One famously acidulous Homeric sceptic, R. C. Jebb, had pointed out that the incident which opens the twentieth book of the *Odyssey* would have been physically impossible at Tiryns. The poem narrates that Odysseus, having finally reached his home island of Ithaca and assumed a beggar's disguise, passed a sleepless night in the vestibule of his palace worrying about what his wife might have been up to during his long absence, his worst fears sharpened by the sight of the wanton women of the household tiptoeing through the space on their way to the men's quarters. Jebb had seized on the fact that there was no apparent means of direct communication between the two sides of the palace at Tiryns to proclaim that this Homeric corridor-creeping could not have taken place. But Tsountas was able to report that what was true of Tiryns turned out to be untrue of Mycenae: 'There we find a door in the north wall of the vestibule leading directly to the women's apartments. Thus in the actual palace of Mycenae, as well as the ideal one at Ithaca, an Odysseus, lying wakeful with his tormenting thoughts, would be right in the track of the guilty women.'

One of the most atmospheric (not to say terrifying) parts of the site excavated by Tsountas is a vertiginous descent of ninety-nine slippery steps right into the darkness of the living rock. The stairs take you from inside the citadel, under the north wall, to a spot deep underground about 40 metres beyond the fortress that once housed a subterranean reservoir (now filled in for safety's sake). It is an impressive bit of ancient engineering; above the steps the sweating stone walls meet in a corbelled vault nearly 4 metres high; near the reservoir the passage is roofed with great horizontal slabs. No trace of its existence is visible from the outside. 'The purpose of this astonishing and truly Cyclopean work is clear,' Tsountas announced. 'As the science of the time was unequal to the task of carrying the water from the lower spring to the acropolis, it was conducted to the most convenient point in the course of its natural flow, where a reservoir had been prepared to receive it and a covered communication with the citadel provided.' This hidden cistern – 'perhaps the fruit of bitter experience' – was designed to protect the water supply in event of siege.

Extensive excavation of the acropolis and the surrounding area enabled Tsountas to reconstruct something of the daily life of the ordinary people of Mycenae. According to his interpretations, the houses inside the citadel were divided into two classes, 'some ... of very shabby construction, others fairly well built ... occupied mainly by masters and menials'. Many of these were two-storey structures, and the dirt floors of the unoccupied lower rooms 'were found to be thickly strewn not only with potsherds, but also with the bones of various animals', provoking the archaeologist to a lecture on the 'not over-nice' table manners of Homeric legend: 'Not only do we see them flinging the bare bones on the floor, but there lie the hoofs of beeves ready to hand when a missile is wanted, and the bloody hides for non-combatants to shield themselves with ...'. He also reconstructs the diet of the slobs of Mycenae: 'We find bones of the swine, goat, sheep, ox, deer, hare ... shells of mussels and other molluscs, but never fishbones.' (It should be noted that Dörpfeld, an architect by training, took issue with this whole reconstruction in the preface to *The Mycenaean Age*, suggesting that the 'lower floors' were foundations and the bones and refuse earlier than the buildings.)

Only after his chapter on the private houses of the city did Tsountas turn to the famous shaft graves. Gently demolishing every aspect of Schliemann's interpretation, Tsountas describes how the shaft graves originally occupied but one small part of a much larger cemetery, far older than the Lion

Gate and the walls and the palace. This cemetery lay *outside* a much smaller earlier citadel, and contained a royal area enclosed by a low circular wall. Long after the period in which the royal tombs were in use, the area was treated with reverence, the position of each grave marked with tombstones. Eventually Mycenae grew so much in prestige and population that the citadel had to be extended. The citadel walls were dismantled and rerouted to where they stand today, built in a curve to accommodate the sacred enclosure. At this time the Lion Gate was built. The ground over the royal tombs was then artificially raised to bring it up to the level of the acropolis entrance, and a new circle was constructed from two concentric rings of thin slabs of pale grey stone, topped with a third slab. So powerful was the tradition of the site's sanctity that even during the successive disasters, desertions and reoccupations that beset the city for the next millennium nothing was ever built there.

As for the great vaulted structures outside the citadel, Tsountas had the good fortune to discover one of the only unplundered hoards of treasure from a Greek beehive tomb. The tomb – located at Vapheio near Sparta – had been discovered and cleared in 1805, but Tsountas found an undisturbed burial in the floor, complete with stunning gold funereal goods, thus proving beyond doubt that these monuments were not royal treasuries but royal graves. With this information in hand, Tsountas was then able to reconstruct for the reader the original magnificence of the greatest of all beehive tombs, Mycenae's so-called Treasury of Atreus, describing the intricately carved limestone pillars that once stood on either side of the entrance, the ornate red porphyry that filled the 'relieving triangle' above the lintel stone, and the great wood and bronze folding doors. From the pattern of nails that were still to be seen protruding from the ascending courses of stone inside the tomb, he hypothesised that the vaulted interior was once decorated with two bands of a frieze, below which the walls were covered in bronze plates and above which they were studded with bronze rosettes. From the main chamber another folding door in a decorated frame opened into a second, alabaster-lined room. 'Such, briefly described, is the Treasury of Atreus', Tsountas remarked, 'but the impression of the structure itself is beyond the power of words' (illustration 14).

By analogy with the extraordinarily fine treasure from the Vapheio tomb, Tsountas invited the reader to fill the Treasury of Atreus and the seven other beehive tombs at Mycenae with grave goods of greater sophistication, if lesser quantity, than the famous shaft-grave gold. The beehive tombs were later than the graves on the acropolis, and the lesser quantity of valuable items in them indicated to the archaeologist that 'with time the view of the future life had begun to grow somewhat more rational …'. This increase in rationality was only relative, however, and Tsountas describes with a certain relish the ritual libations of blood, milk, wine and honey that were poured into the sacrificial pits dug for that purpose in the entrance to the tombs, as well as the 'slaves or captives' that were 'slain on purpose to accompany their master to Hades'.

A chapter on dress and personal adornment traced the evolution of Mycenaean clothes from 'the primitive Aryan breech-cloth' to the Mycenaean lady in all her finery, decked out in soft purple wool and white linen, a gold diadem around her brow and golden ornaments in her dark hair, her skirts

14. There have been many attempts to reconstruct the elaborately decorated entrance to the Treasury of Atreus. In this one, French architect and art historian Charles Chipiez has filled the relieving triangle with a repetitive pattern and placed the lions of Mycenae on either side. All of it is speculative except for the columns flanking the door. So many fragments of these were found that they could be restored in their entirety.

covered in dozens of gold sequins. Male dress had to be reconstructed mainly from the depictions of battle, ranging from the stark-naked defenders shown on a famous siege scene to

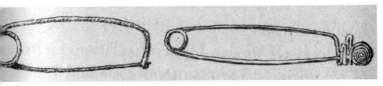

15. Bronze Age safety-pins from Mycenae that make the Mycenaeans seem like a practical, ingenious and, above all, *familiar* sort of people.

the mini-skirted soldiers marching around the Warrior Vase. In this chapter Tsountas also illustrated three examples of an object that would become an iconic artefact of Mycenaean culture, the Bronze Age safety-pin, a little fragment of daily life eloquent of the humanity and ingenuity of these ancient people (illustration 15).

In his chapter on the religion of the Mycenaeans, Tsountas repudiated Schliemann's practice of plastering 'Homeric labels on Mycenaean works' in favour of trying to get the artefacts to speak a 'language of their own'. The vocabulary of the votive objects turned out to be distinctly unHomeric. Tsountas drew the reader's attention to the 'oft-recurring figure of a female with rudely formed arms crossed upon the breast or even clasping a child, often with the *vulva* strongly marked', in whom he saw the 'goddess of generation, call her by what name we will'. By the end of the nineteenth century the theory of a prehistoric stage of matriarchal social organisation was widely accepted, and the presiding deity of Tsountas' Mycenae was a primeval Artemis 'universally worshipped as the great Nature-goddess, queen of men and beasts'. This Artemis was the goddess of life and death, not just 'the sinewy virgin huntress with bow or booty in hand', but also 'the plump matron with full breasts and broad hips that emphasise the maternal function'. Accompanying the Great Mother Goddess was a less important primitive Zeus, brandishing his spear and shield, and a wide array of 'demons of forest, mountain and stream'.

Schliemann had not found any evidence for writing at Mycenae, but Tsountas dug up a small number of objects incised with what were clearly characters of an ancient script. This scanty material had recently been greatly amplified by the indefatigable researches of an English scholar, Arthur Evans, who had amassed a large collection of tiny carved stones, mostly from Crete, that seemed to demonstrate that 'an elaborate system of writing did exist within the limits of the Mycenaean world'. Evans identified two scripts, one pictographic and the other linear. Tsountas suggested that the pictographic script was limited to Crete, never spreading to the mainland or influencing in any way the culture of the Mycenaeans. He acknowledged that the linear script did spread a bit further afield, but the paucity of inscribed artefacts so far found on the mainland – only three from Mycenae and six altogether from continental Greece – suggested to Tsountas that 'The Hellenic stock in Greece who wrought out the Mycenaean civilisation seem not to have required or used any system of writing.'

Although he was wrong about Mycenaean illiteracy, much of what Tsountas deduced from the remains of Mycenae has been borne out by more than a century of subsequent archaeological endeavour, including his insistence that that Mycenae was inhabited by the lineal ancestors of Homeric and classical Greeks, rather than 'immigrants from the Islands or the

Orient'. Unlike his German, French and British contemporaries, Tsountas had no axe to grind about the origin place of this ancient population, shrugging that 'To retrace the course of the Achaean [one of Homer's names for the Greeks] to his proto-ethnic cradle ... is a task for other hands.' But even so the identification of the Mycenaeans as Greek provoked Tsountas into a nationalist outburst, his political passions finally getting the better of his archaeological rigour. For him, the relationship between Mycenae and Troy was best understood as part of a long history of European rivalry with Asia, in which the two cities featured as the ancient equivalents of the great imperial centres of London and St Petersburg: 'The sea power in the Aegean and the land power on the Hellespont could no more avoid an Eastern Question then than can England and Russia to-day.' While Greece continued to slowly expand her borders at the expense of the Turks, the archaeologist sighed over the 'eternal Eastern Question, in which the siege of Troy is a mere episode, as are Marathon and Salamis [decisive battles in the Persian Wars] and Navarino [the naval confrontation that decided the outcome of the Greek War of Independence]'.

In adding the battle of Navarino to a long list of conflicts that began with the Trojan War, Tsountas was merely extending a tradition that had been initiated by Herodotus. More anachronistic and politically dubious was the way in which he and his American co-author recruited the strange and ancient Mycenaean civilisation to the spirit of modern Euro-American liberalism: 'Whoever has mused upon Mycenae', they said, 'even in its ruins, needs no unreined imagination to feel how fitting it was as a point of departure for the struggle with the East. The Achaean capital faces the West; over the lofty mountains at its back the sun rises but late.' And later, in their discussion of the Mycenaean debt to the older civilisations to the east, they flesh out this westward orientation: 'It is not so much technical mastery we admire in the artist as his vigour, his elasticity, his dash, and the untrammelled spirit which never stoops to servile imitation, but looks nature in the face and then registers in forms of art the naïve impression of it.' By the end of the book, they had built to a resounding conclusion: 'The Mycenaean world was of the West, not so much geographically as in its whole spiritual attitude. It was forward looking and forth putting. It had in it the promise and potency of what Europe and America have now wrought out of the complex of modern civilisation.'

The year that the English edition of *The Mycenaean Age* was published, another episode in the 'eternal Eastern Question' came to a bloody climax. An uprising against Ottoman rule on the island of Crete had turned into a disastrous, short-lived war in which the Greek army – still equipped for the independence struggle of seventy years before – was resoundingly defeated by the Sultan's troops. Despite this humiliation, the intervention of the Great Powers secured Cretan autonomy the following year, whereupon the many promising archaeological sites that dotted the coasts and mountains were divided up among French, British and Italian archaeologists like the spoils of empire. Over the next half-century the labours of these archaeological teams revealed a whole ancient world on Crete, uncovering a sophisticated Bronze Age civilisation that was already in its prime when Mycenae was nothing but a crude barbarian outpost.

The real prize of Cretan archaeology – the legendary Palace of Minos at Knossos – went to Arthur Evans, the same English scholar who had been drawn inexorably to the island in pursuit of Mycenaean writing. Already a peppery and idiosyncratic 50-year-old when he began to excavate Knossos, Evans left the stamp of his formidable personality and burning political convictions on the archaeology of ancient Crete. Above all, a streak of diehard romanticism came together with the exigencies of post-Ottoman reconstruction to make of the Minoan world something of a pacifist paradise. Evans had served as a correspondent to the *Manchester Guardian* in the wake of the 1897 war and reported with fairly even-handed revulsion on the terrible Muslim/Christian massacres across eastern Crete. Keen to represent the pagan past as a site of healing and reconciliation, Evans resurrected Bronze Age Crete as an unfortified idyll, internally peaceful under the benign rule of Knossos, and protected from its enemies without by the legendary seafaring skills of King Minos' navy. This pacifism came together with the widely held belief that ancient Crete had at one time been a matriarchy, to make the Minoan Age appear as not only the forerunner to the Mycenaean culture, but also in many respects its polar opposite. Knossos was characterised as feminine where Mycenae was masculine, pacific where it was militaristic, sophisticated where it was rough and decadent when it was young and vigorous (illustration 16).

Tsountas had stopped excavating in 1902 and it would not be until after the Great War that archaeologists once again attacked the citadel of Mycenae, this time at Evans' suggestion. Evans, lording it over his little Bronze Age kingdom, and never afraid to advance an idiosyncratic interpretation, insisted until the end of his life that the Palace of Knossos had been the centre of a vast Minoan empire, a *pax Minoana*

16. This scene engraved on the bezel of a gold signet ring seems to show the Mycenaeans engaged in an outdoor ritual involving the fruit of a sacred tree. The central figure has been variously interpreted as a goddess, a priestess and a worshipper. With her flounced pantaloons, bare breasts and wasp waist, she is dressed exactly like one of the court ladies from the Minoan Palace of Knossos. Many of the signet rings found in Mycenaean burials feature scenes of this kind, attesting to the influence of Minoan cult in Mycenae.

reaching deep into the Greek mainland. After the war he suggested to the British School of Archaeology in Athens that it should reconsider Mycenae 'in view of the great discoveries in Crete which have thrown entirely new light on the origin and development of the Mycenaean civilisation'. In 1920 the archaeologist Alan Wace began the excavation.

Wace, a classical archaeologist by training and an enthusiastic anthropologist by inclination, had spent the years before the Great War scrambling around the remoter fringes of southern Europe and Asia Minor in a Norfolk jacket and plus-fours, studying Greek sculpture and Italian folklore, following round the nomadic shepherds and traders of the Vlach people of the Balkans, collecting Greek embroidery, excavating prehistoric tombs, recording classical inscriptions and photographing remains. In 1914 he was appointed director of the British School at Athens, where he presided over the installation of electric light in the director's house and – more controversially – of women students in the hostel.

The first task of Wace and his team from the British School was to go over some of the already-excavated parts of the site, restudying and redigging the Lion Gate, the Palace, the Grave Circle and the tholos tombs. At the palace the re-examination considerably expanded the ground plan of the building, including the addition of a bathroom with a red stucco floor. By this time Schliemannesque mythical literalism seemed nothing but quaint and folksy, as evidenced by Wace's comment that 'Since the discovery of this bath, modern local tradition at Mycenae has made this the scene of Agamemnon's murder and invoked the red colour as confirmation!' But he undoubtedly still felt the excitement of disinterring the backdrop to the epics, and found himself unable to resist peopling the final centuries of Bronze Age Mycenae with the legendary heroes. In June 1922, for example, he and a small team climbed the steep peak to the north of the citadel and camped overnight, spending the next day checking the site for ancient remains. They found traces of Mycenaean walls. His report ended on an elegiac note: 'here on this steep and waterless limestone peak the lords of Mycenae maintained ... a small fort and look-out station to announce to them by fire or other signals any stirring news – the sudden approach of an enemy, or the fall of Troy.'

Arthur Evans would live to repent of his suggestion to the British School that they reopen the excavations at Mycenae. He had expected that his theory of Minoan dominance over the mainland would be borne out, but instead he encountered stout resistance. Wace had worked closely with the brilliant American archaeologist Carl Blegen, whose excavations at two prehistoric sites north of Mycenae near Corinth had established an independent sequence for mainland culture. He therefore continued to argue that the Mycenaeans had a separate trajectory, culturally dominated by Crete in their early days but politically and militarily ascendant after 1400 BC, with some of their architectural and artistic achievements developing independently of their southern neighbour. Evans could never bring himself to believe any story except that of Minoan colonisation of the mainland from the beginning to the end of Mycenaean history. Trying to bring the Mycenaeans into line with this theory, he published an incendiary little pamphlet (as usual, beautifully bound and expensively produced) arguing that Wace and his team had got it all wrong and that the beehive tombs were actually *earlier* than the shaft graves. Evans argued that the shaft graves were the products of a later, decadent age, into which the treasure from the beehive tombs had been secreted during a siege. In this way both the best building – the Treasury of Atreus – and the most glamorous treasure – the shaft-grave gold – were made contemporary with each other and with the best period of Minoan art and architecture.

Wace stuck to his guns, and in 1923 his excavations at Mycenae were stopped, while his directorship of the British School was not renewed, possibly due to Evans wielding his baleful influence. During the 1920s and 30s, however, Wace had his quiet revenge, as he and Carl Blegen further refined and consolidated their chronology for mainland pottery, thus demolishing Evans' spurious reasoning. In 1939 he was able to return to Mycenae for one more year before the outbreak of war. His team excavated fifteen graves – mostly much shallower than Schliemann's shaft graves – cut into the soft limestone beneath the remains of a cluster of buildings just outside the Lion Gate. Tsountas' theory about the shaft graves being part of a sixteenth and fifteenth-century BC cemetery was now proven correct. Wace also managed, by dint of classifying their architectural techniques and studying the pottery styles associated with each one, to rank the nine extant beehive tombs in order of age. The earliest one, the 'Cyclopean Tomb', either followed closely or overlapped the last of the shaft graves; at least seven or eight of the structures predated the construction of the present fortification walls.

Wace inherited Tsountas' view of Mycenaean religion as a polytheistic cult centring on the worship of a goddess, around whom a younger goddess orbited, as well as a lesser male satellite. In 1939, when he was excavating the palace, the archaeologist discovered the scanty ruins of what he thought must have been a little shrine on the topmost part of the acropolis, containing an artefact that displayed this whole pantheon. One of the most exquisitely naturalistic of all representations of the human form in Mycenaean art, this little ivory sculpture depicts two kneeling women, arms round each other, with a child leaning over the thigh of one, its elbows resting on the knee of the other. The women share a single woven shawl that drapes from the shoulder of one and wraps round the hips of her companion. Wace suggests that it was originally meant to be the decorative pommel of a ceremonial staff or sceptre – the base of the piece is as detailed as the rest – carved in the image of the divinities to which the nearby shrine was dedicated: 'the Great Mother and her younger associate, and their young male companion ...' (illustration 17).

Wace's return to the acropolis of Mycenae was cut short by war. Over on the other side of the Peloponnese, another archaeological team, led by Carl Blegen and Konstantine Kourouniotis, from the Greek Archaeological Service, was enjoying one last season before the cataclysm. A few kilometres north-east of the Bay of Navarino – the site of the famous battle that decided the outcome of the Greek War of Independence – the team had picked out a promising spot on a low hill that they hoped would turn out to be the location of Nestor's Palace. Nestor features in the *Iliad* as Agamemnon's sage advisor, and his domain, 'sandy Pylos', had since antiquity been associated with three different sites in western Greece. After surface explorations in 1938 and 1939, Kourouniotis and Blegen concluded that the upper part of the Englianos ridge near the modern town of Hora

17. The ivory triad found by Alan Wace on the highest point of the acropolis of Mycenae. The two women – again dressed in the tightly tailored and flounced style typical of Minoan Crete – are shown arm-in-arm, sharing a single woven shawl. The toddler was thought by Wace to be a boy, and he accordingly interpreted the group as the holy family of Minoan-Mycenaean religion – Mother, Maid and boy-God. The child is now, on the basis of its costume, thought to be a girl.

might prove to be the right one. On 4 April 1939, with the aid of only one student, Blegen began tentatively to dig. By the end of the day they had uncovered stone walls and a cement floor, fragments of painted plaster and, the greatest prize, five clay tablets incised with the linear script that Evans had identified in Crete and which had been found on a few objects at Mycenae. By an amazing stroke of luck, Blegen's trial trench ran through what became known as the 'archive room', and that first season's work produced no fewer than 600 tablets. The palace's calamity turned out to be the archaeologists' good fortune – the tablets had been baked hard by the great conflagration that had destroyed the buildings. With this confirmation of the use of writing in Mycenaean culture, the main outlines of the Greek Bronze Age had finally emerged from the Peloponnesian soil.

....

THE SWASTIKA AND THE
BUTTERFLY

Schliemann may have been wrong at every turn in his interpretation of the shaft graves, but it was his name that would
be for ever associated with the discovery of the Greek Bronze
Age. In October 1880 he moved his family into a new house
on Panepistimiou Street in Athens, a fitting backdrop for the
immensely grand social life that his fame had now secured.
The Schliemann pile was designed in the neo-classical mode,
its elegant façade pierced by a two-storey loggia, the balus-
trade around the flat roof interrupted by pairs of white marble
statues. Now home to the Numismatic Museum of Athens,
the villa from a distance blends seamlessly with the nineteenth-century university buildings, mansions and embassies
all round it. It is only when you get up close that it becomes
apparent what a magnificently self-important production it
is, covered on nearly every available surface with a bewilder-
ing array of inscriptions, symbols, murals and mosaics, all
bearing the insignia of Schliemann's obsessions (illustration
18).

The first thing that you are likely to notice as you
approach Schliemann's house is that it has a title. In between
the two levels of the loggia a Greek inscription reads Iliou

18. Schliemann's 1880 house in Athens, now the Numismatic Museum.

Melathron, 'Palace of Troy'. Already, the building's pretensions seem faintly ludicrous, as its appearance owes so little to Trojan architecture. It was not until after Arthur Evans had restored the Palace of Knossos in reinforced concrete in the 1920s and 30s that modern architects would attempt to work in a neo-Bronze Age idiom, and even then the style never really caught on. So the only concessions to the actual Trojans to be found on the exterior of Schliemann's Palace are in the detail. Most striking, the building is ringed with swastikas. The basement window bars present dusty rows of the symbol, while the garden railings and front entrance gates wrap their swastikas in a florescence of wrought-iron leaves and blossoms (illustration 19). The only other Bronze Age motif visible from the outside is the fat-bodied butterfly found on many of the gold artefacts in the third shaft grave of Mycenae, which appears as an incongruous note on the Pompeiian-style painted ceiling of the loggia.

Inside, the house is a wonderland of autodidactic eccentricity. Many of the walls are covered with painted Greek inscriptions, consisting of homilies from various ancient Greek writers as well as long passages from Homer on subjects appropriate to the function of the rooms – dancing, dining and the like. Around the walls of one large chamber runs a frieze depicting scenes of naked children – wingless Renaissance *putti* – doing archaeology. One tousle-headed infant raises a lorgnette to his eyes as he peruses an ancient manuscript; another scratches his blond curls as he traces the letters of a carved inscription; elsewhere peachy-buttocked toddlers wrestle vases out of the ground. The mosaic floor of this room is covered with repeated motifs from the excavations, including an owl-headed vase and a two-handled

19. The wrought-iron gates of Schliemann's Athenian mansion. The swastika motif from his Trojan excavations is here embedded in a neo-Pompeiian design of winged sphinxes and acanthus leaves. Thought by Schliemann to be a symbol of the 'Aryan race', the motif is continued in the window bars at street-level.

goblet from Troy, the distinctive outline of an earring from the Mycenaean hoard, and the same plump-thoraxed butterfly from the gold sequins of the third shaft grave. Among the Bronze Age iconography, butterflies and swastikas seem to vie for dominance. The floor of one small, square room consists entirely of swastikas. A mosaic butterfly with a 2-metre wingspan sits at the centre of the floor of the inner hall. Above it on the ceiling, a whimsical Pompeiian fresco incorporates the bizarre image of two naturalistically rendered blue butterflies on what appear to be *leashes*, floating above a white swastika on a black background (illustration 20).

For the post-war visitor, the overall effect of Schliemann's mansion can be disorienting, the swastika appearing in the service of an haute-bourgeois aesthetic almost as alien to the collectivist enthusiasms of the Nazi era as it is false to the Bronze Age. The Iliou Melathron transports us back to the very heart of a vanished time, when racial hierarchies and Aryan ideology were a respectable part of the search for a scientific account of human origins, when Germany and Italy were newly unified and European nationalism was still poised between idealism and atrocity. As the great tide of Christian faith receded, a wave of archaeologically inspired origin myths swept in to replace it, every nation and group racing to rewrite the Book of Genesis in the image of its own interests. Fantasy pagan monuments such as Priam's palace and Agamemnon's tomb became highly politicised projections of a post-Christian future, icons of antiquity that were made to bear all the fears and desires of modernity.

On a different scale, but just as evocative and unnerving as Schliemann's house, is one of the most poignant of pre-war relics, the guestbook of a modest pension in the village of

20. Detail of the fresco on the ceiling of the inner entrance hall of Schliemann's mansion. This proto-surreal, neo-Pompeiian whimsy shows two bright blue butterflies on leashes floating above a white swastika on a black background.

Neo-Mykínes. The Belle Hélène claims to be the place where Schliemann stayed during the excavation of Mycenae; what is certain is that it is the hostel where every distinguished visitor to the ruins stayed in the first half of the twentieth century. Curled photographs of the significant pages of the guestbook adorn the Belle Hélène's lobby. The faded signatures include those of Virginia and Leonard Woolf, Maurice Chevalier, Cecil Beaton, Claude Debussy, Jean-Paul Sartre, Benjamin Britten, Léon Blum, Karl Jung, Stephen Spender, Bertrand Russell and, appearing in three separate years, Joseph Goebbels, Heinrich Himmler and Hermann Göring. The Belle Hélène guestbook is to modernism what Schliemann's Palace of Troy is to the *fin-de-siècle* – an artefact that bears witness to all the tremendous historical excitement and terrifying political innocence of those decades when the butterfly and the swastika existed side-by-side.

Perhaps no one embodies the contradictions of modern Mycenae more perfectly than Gabriele d'Annunzio, the first Nietzsche-inebriated artist to reel away from the site of Schliemann's excavations in a fever of inspiration. D'Annunzio was once Italy's most famous poet, an extravagant libertine and relentless showman whose turn to proto-fascist politics after the Great War has guaranteed his relative posthumous obscurity. In 1895, when the poet was in his early thirties, already celebrated for his inflammatory journalism, stirring lyric gift and careless amatory adventures, he embarked on a Greek cruise. On the trip, d'Annunzio and his companions stopped in Athens and admired the shaft-grave gold before travelling down the coast to the Argolid. At Mycenae, which was baking in the fierce August heat, the poet read Aeschylus and Sophocles under the Lion Gate. Upon his return to Italy d'Annunzio, emboldened by this brush with legend, turned his hand to a new genre, producing his first play rapidly in the autumn of 1896. *The Dead City* is an overwrought neo-Greek tragedy featuring adulterous and incestuous desires among a modern Italian foursome who are stranded over a summer at Mycenae while one of their number excavates the citadel. The play is an oddly static bit of stagecraft, and it is a tribute to d'Annunzio's reputation that the two most famous actresses of the day – Eleanora Duse and Sarah Bernhardt – competed to play the female lead.

The four main characters are the blind, beautiful, long-suffering Anna; her husband, the d'Annunzio-like poetic genius Alessandro; his friend, the archaeological obsessive Leonardo; and Leonardo's sister, the lovely Bianca Maria. Along with Anna's nurse, the four of them are holed up in a villa overlooking the acropolis of Mycenae while Leonardo digs away at the ruins in search of Agamemnon's tomb. It quickly becomes apparent that in the course of their Mycenaean sojourn Alessandro has grown sick of his wife and fallen for Bianca Maria. As d'Annunzio's love life consisted of a series of dilemmas of exactly this shape – how to deal with the present incumbent when his wayward desires fixed on a new object? – it is impossible not to read authorial wish fulfilment in the self-sacrifice of Anna, who notices the mutual attraction between her husband and her friend and willingly abdicates her claim in favour of the other woman. Unfortunately, before Alessandro and Bianca Maria can get off with each other, Leonardo reveals that he too has a crush on his sister, an incestuous obsession so painful that he has to kill her by pushing her face into the legendary spring that gushes out behind the citadel. The play ends with the blind

Anna groping her way up to the spring and running her hands over the wet, dead face of her friend, shrieking as she realises what has been done.

It is the exhumation of Agamemnon and company that is supposed to endow the play with deeper significance, the horrible fate of the ancient protagonists foreshadowing the nasty events unfolding in the present. At the end of the first act, a ridiculous scene has the whole of the contents of the shaft graves emerging in the course of a single afternoon. Alessandro and the two women are peering out at the ruins from the loggia of their villa when they see Leonardo waving frantically from the Lion Gate. A few minutes later he bursts into the house covered in dust and announces that he has found the sepulchres of Agamemnon and his entourage: 'The gold, the gold … the corpses … an immense amount of gold … all the corpses covered in gold …' etc. The two corpses that are described in detail are, of course, Agamemnon, with his open eyes, long straight nose and oval chin, and Cassandra: 'supine on a bed of golden leaves with numberless gold butterflies on her garment, her brow bound with a diadem … a golden pair of scales … upon her breast … her two sons … at her sides like two innocent lambs …'. It is Cassandra who really steals the show and the second act sees both Bianca Maria and Anna fiddling with her stuff and declaiming about her tragic fate. Schliemann's version of the excavations had already sacrificed much to the cause of dramatic effect; in d'Annunzio's hands the muddy, gruelling, sometimes tedious months of the dig were telescoped into a single burning summer day and raised to a pitch of absolute hysteria.

It is no coincidence that d'Annunzio's play takes place in a neo-classical villa, with the Cyclopean walls of the citadel of Mycenae only glimpsed through the serene colonnade of the villa's loggia. The Bronze Age is really no more than decoration for his play, much as the Mycenaean and Trojan symbols are subsumed to the pastiche Renaissance and Pompeiian decor of Schliemann's house in Athens. D'Annunzio was a lifelong Nietzschean, and his attempt to transpose the ghastly themes of ancient Greek drama into a modern key constituted his answer to Nietzsche's call for a new tragic age. His first effort was more swooning *fin-de-siècle* melodrama than modern tragedy, however, and a really Nietzschean Bronze Age, one that had properly shrugged off the pale columns of Victorian Hellenism, had to wait until the twentieth century had turned.

Right on cue, just as Nietzsche died after eleven years of madness and the new century began, a group of Cambridge classicists devoted to Nietzsche, Freud, Durkheim and Schliemann, began to argue that Greek drama and mythology had their roots in struggles between the worshippers of different primitive gods. This modernist Bronze Age distilled archaeology, psychoanalysis, myth studies, feminism and anthropology into a heady exposé of the savagery of the Greeks. As Jane Ellen Harrison, lecturer in classical archaeology at Newnham College and one of the founders of the group, explained in her *Reminiscences of a Student's Life*: 'We Hellenists were, in truth, at that time a "people who sat in darkness," but we were soon to see a great light, two great lights – archaeology and anthropology. I had just left Cambridge when Schliemann began to dig at Troy …' Harrison's hobby horse was the conflict between the old order of matriarchal goddesses and the upstart Olympians and she interpreted the column that rises between the lions above the gate to the Mycenaean citadel as an icon of the Great Mountain Mother, not yet usurped by the patriarchal Zeus.

In 1903 the Austrian poet and playwright Hugo von Hofmannsthal drew on the same fashionable synthesis of archaeology, psychoanalysis and anthropology to portray Agamemnon's vengeful daughter as savage and neurotic. When in 1909 Hofmannsthal's *Elektra* premiered in Dresden as an opera with a score by the ardent Nietzschean Richard Strauss, the props, sets and costumes were based on the excavations at Mycenae. A photograph of the London production of the opera shows the serving women with whom the play opens gathered around a well in the courtyard clutching their Mycenaean vases. The well, a low circular brick edifice, is reminiscent of a structure that Schliemann had found in the Grave Circle: 'an almost circular mass of Cyclopean masonry, with a large round opening in the form of a well … a primitive altar for funeral rites'. Tsountas described it as a 'sacrificial pit … intended to receive the blood of victims slaughtered over it as well as the customary libations', a sort of funnel for delivery of blood and wine to the underworld. No serene colonnades here. Shocked reception of the play and the opera – the critics were alarmed at the way the noble, sublime and luminous Greeks had been bestialised and perverted – demonstrated the extent to which the new Mycenaean primitivism could serve as ammunition against repressed Victorian classicism (illustration 21).

The modernist relationship to the ancient world was one in which the Bronze Age could seem closer to the present and the future than any version of classical antiquity, the very muteness of the remains making it easy for prehistory to speak

21. Before and after modernism. On the left is Frederic Leighton's *Electra at the Tomb of Agamemnon* of 1868, painted a few years before the excavation of Mycenae. This is a typical example of one of Leighton's 'Victorians in togas', standing gracefully mournful by the side of a fluted column. (The Lion Gate appears very tiny in the top right hand corner.) On the right, is the leading lady from a 1910 London production of Richard Strauss' opera *Electra*. In this production – which prided itself on its archaeologically correct costumes and sets based on the excavations at Mycenae and Knossos – the Mycenaean princess has become thoroughly savage and neurotic, with her uncombed hair, clenching fingers and staring eyes.

with the voice of modernity. When Schliemann sent out his dispatches announcing his discovery of the burnt walls of Troy, Agamemnon's Trojan campaign came to seem like a real, almost recent event, reverberating with contemporary concerns. Passages such as this one from Rudolf Virchow's preface to Schliemann's *Ilios* made the prehistoric conflict urgently alive:

> *Here was a great devouring fire, in which the clay walls of the buildings were molten and made fluid like wax, so that congealed drops of glass bear witness at the present day to the mighty conflagration … It was here where Asia and Europe for the first time encountered in a war of extermination (in völkerfressendem Kampfe); it was here that the only decisive victory was won in fight, which the West gained over the East on the soil of Asia, during the whole time down to Alexander the Great.*

As Darwinism and Marxism took over from Christianity as the reigning ideologies of the West, wars of extermination came more and more to be seen as the necessary and often desirable natural outcomes of struggle and competition between nations, a not un-Greek conception of the *agon* of armed conflict horribly transposed to the machine age. Europe filled up with neurasthenic young scholars, innocent of the horrors of combat, marshalling archaeological evidence in the support of their dreams of blood and empire. War was repeatedly proclaimed as physically and morally desirable, an antidote for decadence and a prescription for spiritual renewal. One example will suffice to stand for many – d'Annunzio's classically inflected after-dinner speech on the occasion of Italy's entry into the Great War:

The tenth Muse, Energy ... does not love measured words, she
loves an abundance of blood ... She counts the forces, the nerves,
the sacrifices, the battles, the wounds, the torments, the corpses
... She computes the flesh laid low, the sum of nourishment
offered to the earth so that, digested, it may be converted into
ideal matter, rendered into perennial spirituality. She takes the
horizontal body of a man as the only measure for measuring the
vaster destiny.

When the Balkan Wars of 1912 and 1913 escalated into
the Great War, a Herodotean vision of endless East–West
struggle reaching right back to Agamemnon's assault on Troy
came to seem more and more compelling. In 1915, during the
disastrous Gallipoli campaign, fought against the Germans
and their Turkish allies on the ancient Trojan Plain, newspaper reports routinely referred to the Homeric as well as
the modern Turkish names of the sites. This blood-soaked
topography – greatly indebted to Schliemann and his successors – provoked one anonymous war correspondent to *The
Times* to these anguished reflections on the traumatic repeti-
tions of history:

Graved and scored with characters through all recorded time,
[the map of Europe] is being graved and scored once more, by a
pen of iron and with ink of blood, in characters that seen indel-
ible ... Are our minds the same abiding stuff, on which a God
who is only a God of battles eternally writes his crimson script,
only erasing the message of one age to write it in the next with
a direr pen, dipped still more deep, a message still more charged
with the ancient woe?

The classically educated young men who went to meet the horrors of the war at Gallipoli were irresistibly reminded of the *Iliad*. Rupert Brooke scribbled a fragment of verse on his last voyage, which captured the widespread sense that the ghosts of Troy were once more afoot: 'They say Achilles in the darkness stirred / And Priam and his fifty sons / Wake all amazed, and hear the guns …'. Archaeological excavation had come together with modern warfare to resurrect a very Homeric deity, 'a God who is only a God of battles', inscribing his nightmare epic across the maps and minds of Europe 'by a pen of iron and with ink of blood'.

After the Great War, the realisation that industrial-scale warfare was not in fact a delicious tonic for national well-being created the perfect market for Oswald Spengler's 1919 *Decline of the West*, a two-volume bestseller of intimidating density and sweep. Spengler was a retired schoolteacher whose literary adherence to Nietzsche's warrior creed was in striking contrast to his actual physical condition – weepy, myopic, headache-ridden and consumptive, he was twice declared unfit for military service and spent the years of the war in monkish isolation scribbling away at his magnum opus. *The Decline of the West* was a hugely ambitious piece of work. Spengler hoped for nothing less than to discern in the whole story of Western civilisation historical patterns that would allow him to predict the future. His prophetic framework was Darwinian: he argued that nations, peoples, cities and cultures followed organic patterns of birth, growth, decline and death. The great virtue of the work lay in Spengler's ability to synthesise enormous amounts of information, compressing whole tomes of archaeology and history into single punchy paragraphs. Nowhere was this more apparent than in his treatment of Mycenae:

About the middle of the second millennium before Christ, two worlds lay over against one another on the Aegean Sea. The one, darkly groping, big with hopes, drowsy with the intoxication of deeds and sufferings, ripening quietly towards its future, was the Mycenaean. The other, gay and satisfied, snugly ensconced in the treasures of an ancient culture, elegant, light, with all its great problems far behind it, was the Minoan of Crete.

Spengler repeatedly made an analogy between this relationship and another, later one in the ancient world: 'I see it before me,' he announced, 'the humility of the inhabitants of Tiryns and Mycenae before the unattainable *esprit* of life in Cnossus, the contempt of the well-bred of Cnossus for the petty chiefs and their followers, and withal a secret feeling of superiority in the healthy barbarians, like that of a German soldier in the presence of the elderly Roman dignitary'. From there it was an easy step to reaffirm the essentially Teutonic nature of Mycenaean culture: 'that which stands on the hills of Tiryns and Mycenae is *Pfalz* [domain of a feudal overlord] and *Burg* [hill fort] of root-Germanic type …'

Those Germans who persisted in regarding war as therapeutic would take a less fatalistic comfort from their ancestral connection with the Mycenaeans. In 1920 the swastika made its first appearance in Munich as the emblem of the National Socialist German Workers' Party. The following year the German prehistorian Otto Grabowski published *The Secret of Swastikas and the Cradle of the Indo-Germanic Race*, which celebrated Schliemann's swastikas, then on display in Berlin, but went far beyond the archaeologist in arguing for a Germanic rather than an Asian homeland for the Aryan race. Grabowski's book ended on a triumphant note as he ringingly declared that the winter of the German people was soon to yield to a 'morning, which approaches under the light of the swastika'. In 1923 the philologist-turned-archaeologist Gustaf Kossinna (whose volume on German archaeology went to nine editions, the seventh of which was prefaced by Adolf Hitler) published a two-volume work *Origin and Diffusion of the Germans in Pre- and Early History*, also arguing that Mycenaean civilisation had a Germanic origin. By the time of Hitler's ascendancy, a Teutonic Mycenae had been completely assimilated into the crackpot mixture of archaeology, mythography and so-called 'racial science' that provided German fascism with its own tailor-made prehistory. Accordingly, Himmler, Goebbels and Göring all made their pilgrimages to the site of the legendary city to admire the handiwork of the very first Nazi supermen, the Germanic warriors who had fought and won the first 'war of extermination', and left molten the stones of Troy.

In the 1930s Schliemann himself was fashioned by the Nazis into one of their own, in the image of a Nietzschean *Übermensch*. Although superficially he was a rather unlikely candidate for this role, being small, wiry and owlish, with a drooping moustache, pale domed forehead and a perpetual look of anxiety in his short-sighted eyes, Schliemann's sheer determination had in fact made his body as well as his memory freakishly strong. He gloried in the physical stamina that saw him through the hardships of successive seasons in the field and prodigious feats of authorship, and nurtured it by swimming every morning, rising before dawn to ride out to the nearest body of water in defiance of weather and season (a habit ruefully recalled by his long-suffering offspring). The first authorised biography of Schliemann, Emil

Ludwig's *Schliemann of Troy: the story of a gold seeker*, turned out to be insufficiently celebratory, however, and in 1933 it was burned in Berlin. An idealised portrait was then commissioned by a Nazi official in Mecklenburg, and a teacher at one of Schliemann's old schools, Ernst Meyer, was engaged to write a flattering biography and to edit the archaeologist's letters in such a way as to portray him as an authentic modern German hero. Meyer wrote of his predecessor, Ludwig, who happened to be Jewish, that he 'lacked the organ to detect the German in Schliemann'.

The occupants of the Mycenaean tombs were not only celebrated as proto-Nazis, however. Another interpretation went haring off in the opposite direction, reconstructing the three female occupants of the third shaft grave as the practitioners of an ecstatic nature religion originating in the peaceful, matriarchal society of Bronze Age Crete. After the excavation of Knossos got underway, the objects from the third grave – that jungly profusion of golden leaves, spirals, cuttlefish, star-flowers, serpents, butterflies, griffins, palm-trees, stags, swans, eagles, sphinxes, bare-breasted women and lions – were easily interpreted as votive artefacts belonging to a Minoan cult of the goddess. In 1924 Arthur Evans published an article in which he claimed to have unlocked the religious secrets of the third shaft grave's long-dead inhabitants. Assembling a tiny selection of the artefacts – one of the discs with a butterfly on it, a pair of gold scales with butterflies embossed on the pans and a series of little bullet-shaped objects on chains that he interpreted as chrysalises – he reconstructed a Bronze Age cult of the soul's immortality as symbolised by the butterfly. Mangled remnants of this tradition had survived, he claimed, in the perennially popular fable of Cupid and his butterfly-winged beloved Psyche.

The following year the article was reprinted as a separate pamphlet, a copy of which found its way into the eager hands of the poet and novelist Hilda Doolittle. H.D., plucked from a Pennsylvania backwater by Ezra Pound when she was a beautiful, gawky teenager and subsequently whisked off to London to become a poet, had made her name with a series of stripped-down lyrics on Greek themes. Often writing in the guise of female practitioners of ancient pagan rituals, she had turned herself into the pre-eminent muse of classically inclined ex-pat modernists, a living incarnation of the spirit of primitive Greece. Inspired by Evans' reconstructed cult of the butterfly soul, she began to work butterfly and chrysalis imagery into her poetry and prose. In the autobiographical novel which she began to write soon after the publication of Evans' article, for example, she narrated the story of a teenage nervous breakdown as a modernist Psyche fable, an overwrought bit of self-mythologising which her descent into the underworld of madness and re-emergence into the upper air of sanity followed the archetypal metamorphosis of caterpillar–chrysalis–butterfly.

In 1933 H.D. went to Vienna to undergo a course of psychoanalysis with Sigmund Freud. She found the venerable psychoanalyst, then 77 years old, surrounded by an extensive collection of archaeological artefacts and a comprehensive archaeological library, including Schliemann's *Ilios* and a complete set of Arthur Evans' *Palace of Minos*. Freud regarded psychoanalysis itself as a form of excavation. In the case history that he characterised as his 'first full-length analysis of a hysteria', he compared his procedure 'of clearing away the pathogenic psychical material layer by layer', to 'the technique of excavating a buried city'. In an 1899 letter to his closest friend, Wilhelm Fleiss, Freud confessed that 'I gave myself a present, Schliemann's *Ilios*, and greatly enjoyed the account of his childhood. The man was happy when he found Priam's treasure, because happiness comes only with the fulfilment of a childhood wish.' Later that same year he explicitly identified with Schliemann's triumphalist account of his discoveries, saying that his success in getting a patient to recall an important childhood memory was 'as if Schliemann had once more excavated Troy'.

Over the next forty years Freud worked and reworked his archaeological metaphor for psychoanalysis, often deploying it to reassure his readers that his sometimes rather wild reconstructions of his patients' childhood memories were no more tendentious than archaeological reconstructions of frescoes or vases. In 1895 he began to collect archaeological souvenirs, beginning with plaster replicas of famous classical sculptures but quickly moving on to original artefacts from ancient Greece and Rome (eventually supplemented with pieces from India and China). By the time H.D. blew into his office in the spring of 1933 Freud had over 3000 objects in his collection, a veritable little archaeological museum, crowded into a series of glass cases ranged along the walls of his consulting room.

Freud and H.D. were both ecstatic to have found in each other a fellow archaeological enthusiast, and in the first few weeks of the analysis – which took place five times a week, paid for by H.D.'s sugar-mama and sometime lover 'Bryher' (the shipping heiress Winifred Ellerman) – they had a series of conversations about Crete, Greece and Egypt. This passionate archaeological rapport culminated in one of the psychoanalyst's more bizarre diagnoses. On 23 March H.D. wrote to Bryher that

> *He also cheered me up one day by saying that my special kind of 'fixation' was not known till three years ago, so perhaps it is as well that I was not analysed some ten years back, as I always feel I should be ... or twenty years back. F. says mine is the absolutely FIRST layer, I got stuck at the earliest pre-OE stage and 'back to the womb' seems to be my only solution. Hence islands, sea, Greek primitives and so on.*

The poet's 'special fixation' had been defined by Freud in a 1931 article on 'Female Sexuality' in which he declared that his discovery of the feminine pre-Oedipal stage had 'come as a surprise, like the discovery of the Minoan-Mycenaean civilisation behind the civilisation of Greece'. In his diagnosis of H.D., and later in his 1939 book *Moses and Monotheism*, Freud made far more literal the link between the archaeological and the psychoanalytic strata, resurrecting the deeply eccentric theory of inherited memory that he had first outlined in *Totem and Taboo* twenty years earlier. According to this theory, the matriarchal Minoan civilisation and the patriarchal Mycenaean society that succeeded it had somehow *laid down* the psychic strata of the pre-Oedipal stage and its father-dominated successor. It followed that H.D.'s love of Minoan iconography was no more than a symptom of her mother fixation. For the father of psychoanalysis, the occupants of the Mycenaean shaft graves were not just buried in the rock of the north-eastern Peloponnese, but also, in some mysterious way, embedded in the psyche of every European.

H.D., meanwhile, had moved back to London, where she relieved the stress of the Blitz with a mixture of spiritualist séances and prodigious literary output. Between 1942 and 1944 she composed a trilogy of long poems in which the butterfly deity from the third shaft grave appeared in the guise of Psyche, mother-archetype of the female visionary, avatar of the new Aquarian age and emblem of feminine defiance in the face of the insanity of military conflict: 'she is not shut up in a cave / like a Sibyl; she is not / imprisoned in leaden bars / in a coloured window; / she is Psyche, the butterfly, / out of the cocoon … the counter-coin-side / of primitive terror; / she is not-fear, she is not-war …'. At the same time as the swastika-wielding warriors of the Mycenaean age were being celebrated as the ancestors of the Nazi bombers of London, their female counterparts were being honoured as the embodiment of peace.

In all these responses to Mycenae can be discerned the influence of Friedrich Nietzsche, the erstwhile classics professor whose oracular reading of the *Iliad* delved into the pagan past in order to predict the post-Christian future. Nietzsche was the prototypical modernist exile, a rootless and lonely wanderer who declared himself most at home in ancient Greece. For the Greeks, by contrast, the Hellenic past did not exist in isolation as an unmoored archetype of human brilliance, but was instead powerfully anchored in place and time, a symbol of homecoming and continuity. In the work of one of Greece's greatest modernist poets, the Nobel Laureate George Seferis, the heroes of Homeric legend appear alongside lesser-known aspects of the Greek poetic tradition, embedded in a landscape and woven into a history through which the local and the universal seem effortlessly to illuminate one another.

Seferis himself was wearily familiar with the conditions of exile. Born Georgios Seferiades in 1900 in the western Turkish city of Smyrna (now Izmir), a cosmopolitan, polyglot port where Orthodox Christian Greeks rubbed shoulders with Muslims, Jews, Armenians and western Europeans, he was tossed from place to place – from Smyrna to Athens to Paris to Cairo to Jerusalem – by the capricious tides of twentieth-century politics. He shared with his contemporaries that sense of traumatic repetition so characteristic of the modernist engagement with antiquity, but his was deepened and sharpened by the facts of his nationality and his profession. Seferis was a diplomat, and his awareness of the continuity between past and present was profoundly rooted in his involvement with the political crises that afflicted Greece during his tenure in the Greek Ministry of Foreign Affairs.

In 1935 Seferis evoked the brooding atmosphere at the ruins of Mycenae to pass a veiled comment on current events. In November of that year, after a period of severe political instability, the monarchy was restored in Greece. For Seferis, an ardent republican, this was an appalling development, and he regarded with foreboding the prospect of the total erosion of democracy in his beloved native land. In his poem 'Mycenae', he laments the centuries-long pain of the Greeks, giving voice to his horror at the return of the monarchy by analogy with King Agamemnon's ill-fated homecoming.

... I
who've followed so many times
the path from killer to victim
from victim to punishment
from punishment to the next murder,

groping
the inexhaustible purple
that night of the return
when the Furies began whistling
in the meager grass –
I've seen snakes crossed with vipers
knotted over the evil generation
our fate.

The poem ends with two lines that link the impossible antiquity of the site with the country's long history of dispossession: 'Not even the silence is now yours / here where the millstones have stopped turning.'

The next few years would only confirm the poet's premonition of disaster. General Ioannis Metaxas, leader of the tiny right-wing Party of Free Opinion, was charged by the king with forming a government and in 1936 he dissolved parliament and suspended the constitution. By 1938 the Metaxas regime had openly declared itself a dictatorship, was starting to set up concentration camps for political dissidents and was hailing the advent of the 'Third Greek Civilisation' in imitation of the Nazi Third Reich.

In 1939, as the political situation worsened, Seferis and a friend – the great champion of Greek literature George Katsimbalis – showed their country to a visiting American writer. The two men were rewarded for their hospitality by starring in one of the most passionate travel memoirs ever penned. Henry Miller was 47 when he left Paris in 1939, forced out of his adopted city by the exigencies of war. His intention was to spend a few months on the island of Corfu with his friend Lawrence Durrell before joining a Tibetan monastery.

He ended up staying in Greece for five glorious months, his first and last real holiday, remembered in his memoir *The Colossus of Maroussi* (the colossus of the title being George Katsimbalis), which he wrote upon his return to New York. The book is an extravagant celebration of Greece and the Greeks, a hyperbolic hymn of praise that documents Miller's awakening to a great 'peace of the heart' – an acceptance of the grace and pain of the world, made all the more necessary by the gathering storm of war. 'Standing in Agamemnon's tomb' he announces at the end of the book, 'I went through a veritable rebirth.'

Miller was an admirer of Oswald Spengler's *Decline of the West* and his Mycenae is Spengler's writ large, amplified into a twelve-page torrent of prose whose histrionic intensity manages to be brilliantly evocative of the atmosphere of the site: 'It wears an impenetrable air: it is grim, lovely, seductive and repellent. What happened here is beyond all conjecture. The historians and the archaeologists have woven a slim and altogether unsatisfactory fabric to cover the mystery.' Although Miller insists that the scholars can tell him nothing about the place and boasts a number of times throughout the book that he has never read Homer, Spengler and the tragedians stand him in pretty good stead: 'the same Aegean race which brought the seeds of culture from Crete to Tiryns, here evolved to a godlike grandeur, threw out a quick spawn of heroes, Titans, demigods, and then, as if exhausted and dazzled by the unprecedented and divine-like flowering, relapsed into a dark and bloody intestinal conflict which lasted for centuries ...'. Climbing towards the ruins, 'the blood thickens', he observes, 'the heart slows down, the mind comes to rest obsessively on the shuddering image of a chain of assassinations'. Creeping round the deserted citadel just after sunrise, 'like a cockroach crawling about amidst dismantled splendours', he wonders if the inhabitants of the New World are going the same way as the Mycenaeans, consumed and destroyed by their own crimes, destined to be 'swallowed up' and to leave no trace 'save these ruins, the scattered relics in museums, a sword, an axle, a helmet, a death mask of beaten gold'.

Miller refuses to descend the stairs to the subterranean cistern 'down into that slimy well of horrors', dragging Katsimbalis away from the entrance where 'the heavy roof is buckling with the weight of time'. Instead they walk out of the Lion Gate, over the 'little bridge above the sundered vault of Clytemnestra's resting place', and then down the road to the Treasury of Atreus. It is here, in the most impressive building at the site, that Miller experiences his epiphany, assuming (incorrectly) that this must be where Schliemann discovered the gold-masked bodies. He presents the threshold of the vault as a spiritual knife-edge, on either side of which two different destinies await him: 'I am outside, between the Cyclopean blocks which flank the entrance to the shaft. I am still the man I might have become, assuming every benefit of civilisation to be showered upon me ...' Hesitating a moment before crossing underneath the enormous lintel stone, he feels himself expand into the possibilities of this privileged existence: 'I am blown to the maximum, like a great bowl of molten glass hanging from the stem of a glass-blower ...' One moment he stands outside the tomb, 'the most beautiful, the most cultured, the most marvellously fabricated soul on earth', the next instant everything has changed: 'I am going to put my foot over the threshold – *now*. I do so. I hear nothing.

I am not even there to hear myself shattering into a billion splintered smithereens. Only Agamemnon is there.'

As Miller tells the story of his crossing the threshold of the beehive tomb into his future as 'a spiritual nobody', he expounds on another boundary between two worlds:

They call it Agamemnon's tomb. Well, possibly someone called Agamemnon was here laid to rest. What of it? Am I to stop there, gaping like an idiot? I do not … I say the whole world, fanning out in every direction from this spot, was once alive in a way that no man has ever dreamed of. I say there were gods that roamed everywhere, men like us in form and substance, but free, electrically free. When they departed this earth they took with them the one secret which we shall never wrest from them until we have made ourselves free again. We are to know one day what it is to have life eternal – when we have ceased to murder. Here at this spot, now dedicated to the memory of Agamemnon, some foul and hidden crime blasted the hopes of man. Two worlds lie juxtaposed, the one before, the one after the crime. The crime contains the riddle, as deep as salvation itself.

In *The Colossus of Maroussi* Miller narrates his whole sojourn in Greece as an extended meditation on the riddles of Greek history, and, by extension, the puzzle of human violence. 'The ancient Greek was a murderer … He was at war with everyone including himself. Out of this fiery anarchy came the lucid, healing metaphysical speculations which even today enthral the world.' Solving the puzzle was an urgent matter in 1940, as Miller was clear that everything would change in the onrushing war: 'The next time we meet, any of us, it will be on the ashes of all that we once cherished.' Born in 1891, he was both a child of his time – mildly anti-Semitic, his attitudes towards women oscillating between chivalry and misogyny – but also a prophet of the pacifist counter-culture that would eventually hail him as one of their own. Miller's Mycenae is bloodthirsty and heroic, but he celebrates it as a magnificent cosmic error, the site of fragile civilisation's first fall into the abyss of violence, 'the high slope whence man, having attained his zenith, slipped back and fell into the bottomless pit'.

Just as the Persian Wars and the Peloponnesian War made the historians and dramatists of antiquity look afresh at the story of Troy, so the Eastern Question, the Balkan Wars and the Great War sent people back to Mycenae, seeking explanations and justifications, looking to recruit the ancient heroes to the conflicts of modernity. Whether proclaimed as a prefiguration of Teutonic imperial triumphs, celebrated as the earliest Greek victory over the infidel or reviled as the first hideous crime of civilised man, Agamemnon's Trojan campaign supplied the perfect prehistory for the bloody battlefields and the burned cities of the twentieth century's first half. The heroic warrior ideal was not, however, destined to survive the cataclysm of the Second World War. In April 1941 the Germans launched an invasion of Greece; by June the whole country was under combined German, Italian and Bulgarian occupation. One of the first symbolic gestures of resistance to fascist rule was the tearing down of the Nazi swastika from the Acropolis of Athens on 31 May 1941. The German fantasy of the Aryan Greek had been consumed by its own violence.

8

A CITY WITHOUT HEROES

At the beginning of the twenty-first century, the cult of the hero must be said to be in pretty bad shape. Schliemann has been knocked off his pedestal, Homer has disappeared from the curriculum, Agamemnon has been tried as a war criminal and Mycenae has become politically correct. Garbled versions of the heroic narratives of the late nineteenth century still circulate, enthusiastically recycled by bloggers sharing experiences of their holidays in Greece, but they are increasingly vague and skimpy, a membrane of half-truths stretched thinner and thinner over the burgeoning archaeological and archival evidence.

Since the opening of the Museum of Mycenae in 2003, the gulf between the folktales of Bronze Age archaeology and the current scholarly understanding of the site has become perilously wide. There is a palpable air of bafflement in the first room of the museum, where visitors – who may have prepared themselves for the ruins by groping around in their minds for half-remembered stories of Schliemann kissing the face of Agamemnon and the odd bloodthirsty detail from Greek mythology – stand gaping at the information panel introducing the site. 'Mycenaean Palace civilisation', they learn, had, by the end of the fifteenth century BC, 'reached a highly sophisticated level of state organisation, production methods, literacy and trade'. This achievement was made possible by the 'combined, although hardly co-ordinated efforts of the palaces, whose relations were peaceful and friendly'. Proof of this cooperation comes from 'the character of the culture itself, which was the result of constant and unhindered interplay of cross influences and had attained a cultural unity impossible in a country rent by hostilities'. In the process of consolidating itself into this 'community of cult and customs' the Mycenaean world 'assimilated several diverse tribes, races and regional cultures, primitive as well as advanced, and merged them into a homogeneous whole'. Scholars have given this achievement a name: 'the Mycenaean Koinê', *koinê* being a Greek word meaning 'community' or 'public'. 'The Koinê was the paramount achievement of the Achaeans: it did more than trade commodities and exchange ideas. It created a nation.'

How on earth did Tsountas' 'frowning castles', built, in Mycenae's case, 'not for defence but for aggression', turn into the prosperous, peaceful, friendly, cooperative, multi-cultural Koinê? The answer is that every archaeological development since the Second World War has conspired in the gradual redefinition of Mycenae. Take, for example, the most dramatic breakthrough of the period, the 1953 decipherment of the Mycenaean script Linear B as an archaic form of Greek. The scribes of Linear B turned out to be accountants and bureaucrats, not poets, historians or war correspondents, and the activities that are memorialised in the tablets are those of production and taxation rather than the stirring deeds of battle. Once the contemporary tablets could be read, the famous Homeric epics – composed, after all, at least 400 years too late – became inadmissible evidence for the character of the Bronze Age. Without any bards to celebrate their deeds, the warriors have perforce fallen a bit quiet.

The decipherment of Linear B and the consequent replacement of heroes by bureaucrats happened to fit nicely with a broad reform movement in the discipline as a whole. At the Nuremberg trials, the whole edifice of racial science was toppled, bringing down with it the Aryan Greeks as ancestors of everything wonderful. This resulted in a cascade of changes and reforms across all of Aegean archaeology, a process that has only quickened since the post-colonial convulsions of the 1960s. One clear outcome is that Mycenae has long since ceased to be a bastion of white power or emblem of Western superiority, and talk of 'the Greek race' has been quietly replaced by discussion of the ancient speakers of the Greek language. As befits a post-colonial institution, the Museum of Mycenae is entirely the work of Greek archaeologists, and the projected image of the Mycenaeans as 'creating a nation' may partly express their patriotic pride at a site whose interpretation was for so long dominated by foreigners (illustration 22).

The 'scientising' of excavation has played a subtle part in the same democratising, pacifying process. Prehistoric archaeology has become, belatedly but excruciatingly, aware of all that it cannot know, and syllogisms rehearsing this humbling constraint are dutifully committed to memory by students of the New Archaeology. The laboratory has usurped the library as the principal off-site locus of archaeological investigation, and Mycenae's great epics and dramas have yielded to geological analysis, bioanthropological measurement and the chemistry of food residues. In line with these changes, archaeological practice has a far more communal nature than

22. Post-modern patriotic architecture on the Peloponnese occasionally takes on a Bronze Age flavour, as exemplified by this neo-Mycenaean National Bank in the main square in Nauplion. Note the 'relieving triangle' above the doorway and the downward-tapering columns.

before, with teams of experienced archaeologists working alongside their students and sharing the credit of publication, a democratisation of the work itself that discourages the individualistic heroics of the past.

There is also the question of the quality of the artefacts. As the soil gradually empties and the museums fill up, humbler and humbler objects receive more and more loving attention from their excavators. This has resulted in far greater visibility for the everyday arts of the ordinary people of Mycenae, while 'elite items' such as the shaft-grave treasure now have to take an analytical back seat, routinely dismissed as unrepresentative of the Mycenaean masses. The combined effect of all these factors has been nothing less than revolutionary. Mycenae is no longer peopled with Homeric kings and heroes, but rather crowded with farmers, potters, traders, weavers and artisans, the protagonists of a rational archaeology of ordinary daily life.

Above all, it was the Linear B tablets that made visible the unheroic day-to-day business of the heroic age. Like that other famous decipherment, the exactly contemporaneous elucidation of the double-helical structure of DNA, Linear B was cracked using technologies and insights developed during the Second World War. Before 1939 it was generally believed that an unknown script in an unknown language would surely require a bilingual or multilingual inscription to unlock it. The Egyptian hieroglyphs, to take the most famous example, only yielded their secrets once the Rosetta stone was discovered. During the war pioneering cryptanalytical methods developed under the pressure of military necessity made it clear that given a sufficient quantity of material, any secret code or unreadable script was theoretically crackable using a systematic method of analysis designed to tease out underlying patterns and regularities.

There are, broadly speaking, three forms of writing – pictographic, syllabic and alphabetic. Pictographic scripts, requiring a different symbol for every word, will have the largest number of signs. Syllabic scripts break down words into their constituent sounds, thereby requiring many fewer signs. Alphabetic scripts take this process of economy even further by breaking sounds down into their separate elements. The Linear B texts consist of single signs standing alone, plus groups of signs linked by small vertical bars. It was obvious from the beginning that the single signs were probably pictograms – often recognisable – and that the groups of signs were words written in an either syllabic or alphabetical script. One of the most straightforward results of the statistical method was the conclusion that Linear B is a syllabary, as it has about a hundred signs, which is too many for an alphabet and too few for a pictographic script.

Starting in 1943, the cryptanalytical method was applied to Linear B by the American academic Dr Alice Kober, who, in lieu of a computer, began her analysis by cutting more than 186,000 5cm by 8cm note cards from exam books, greeting cards, envelopes and church flyers salvaged from wartime paper shortages. Kober's questions were deceptively simple. Was the language inflected? Was there a consistent means of denoting a plural? Did it distinguish genders? As she shifted around her thousands of cards, she was able to discern what seemed to be variations in the endings of the same words, the first clues as to the grammar of the language of Linear B. Unfortunately the cigarettes whose packets constituted her filing system killed her in 1950, at the age of 43, before she was able to continue and complete the work.

In 1951 the tablets from Pylos were published, making possible for the first time a really significant statistical analysis of the frequency of the occurrence of every sign. The young British architect Michael Ventris, a brilliant linguist blessed with a remarkable visual memory and an infinite capacity for taking pains, began, in his free time from his job at the Ministry of Education, to crunch the numbers. Gradually, aspects of the language began to emerge. Variations in the endings of words, for example, could be tentatively interpreted as noun declensions; pure vowel signs could be identified; conjunctions became apparent; masculine and feminine endings became visible. Ventris began to draw up grids with five vowels along one axis and fifteen consonants along the other, arranging and rearranging the symbols of Linear B in the resulting field in order to identify the five pure vowel signs and the eighty-plus vowel–consonant combinations that made up the script. Linear B resembles and is related to an ancient Cypriot syllabary, which had been deciphered in the 1870s with the help of bilingual inscriptions. By juggling the seven signs that seemed to be common to the two scripts, plus his grids, Ventris was able to begin to assign sounds to the symbols of Linear B.

The next step for Ventris was to try out various ancient languages to see if any fit with the faint sounds and the intimations of grammar that were beginning to emerge from his grids. Here Arthur Evans' posthumous dominance over the discipline of Aegean archaeology impeded progress towards the solution. Linear B tablets had been found in great numbers only at Knossos and at Pylos. Evans' conviction that the ancient Minoans were the dominant power in the whole region meant that Ventris understood his task as that of identifying the *Minoan* language, the language of the Knossos court, rather than the tongue of the Mycenaean mainlanders spoken at Pylos. It went without saying that the Cretans had to be the ones who had exported their literacy to the Greeks. Ventris' favourite candidate for the language of the tablets was ancient Etruscan, an eminently reasonable guess, as one tradition had the Etruscans arriving in Italy from the Aegean. The possibility that the language of the Knossos tablets might be written in an ancient dialect of Greek, a language with northern roots spoken by the upstart barbarians of Mycenae, was dismissed by him early on as 'based of course upon a deliberate disregard of historical plausibility'.

In 1951, however, Ventris tinkered around with the Greek hypothesis, circulating his results in a paper that he introduced as nothing more than 'a frivolous digression'. In this sheaf of notes he detailed the puzzling fit between what he had already deduced about Linear B and certain Greek words and place names, but hastened to add at the end that he suspected 'this line of decipherment would sooner or later come to an impasse, or dissipate itself in absurdities'. In fact, as he experimented with it further, the 'Greek chimera' refused to fade away. Slowly and methodically, as Ventris forced the mute signs to speak, one Greek word after another, some of them still in use in the markets of Heraklion and the cafés of Nauplion, uttered itself. After a certain point the solution reached critical mass. New signs could be identified by their place in recognisable words, and this value could then be tested elsewhere. The Greek of the Linear B tablets was archaic, mangled, abbreviated, but Greek none the less, the recognisable ancestor of the language of Homer and Aeschylus.

In 1952 Ventris recruited the Cambridge philologist John Chadwick to help with the reconstruction of the archaic dialect and the following year the two men published their canonical 'Evidence for Greek Dialect in the Mycenaean Archives'. Even before the paper was published, many potential sceptics were won over by a dramatic confirmation of the decipherment that came from newly excavated tablets from Pylos. These documents, dug up in 1952 but not cleaned and studied until the following year, featured an ideogram picturing a three-legged pot accompanied by a word that spelled, using Ventris' system, ti-ro-po, i.e. tripod or tripos. By the summer of 1955 Chadwick and Ventris had completed the manuscript of their volume of translated tablets, *Documents in Mycenaean Greek*. The triumphant appearance of the book was completely overshadowed by Ventris' tragic death, at the age of 34, in a car accident a few weeks earlier.

Widespread acceptance of the main outlines of Ventris' system did not mean that the Linear B tablets immediately yielded all their secrets. There were false starts and reversals, controversies and bitter disputes. Many positive translations have since been overturned, and some of the issues remain unresolved even now, fifty years later. The broad outlines are, however, clear. Linear B represents the adaptation by mainlanders of the syllabic Cretan script Linear A (as yet untranslatable) to write an archaic form of Greek. Its presence at Knossos attests to the fact, so long suspected by Alan Wace and his supporters and so long disputed by Evans and his fellow-travellers, that at some point in the fifteenth century BC the Mycenaeans had taken over the greatest of Cretan palaces and become the dominant Aegean power. The last Palace of Knossos, the one that Evans so lovingly restored as the showpiece of his Minoans, actually reflects Mycenaean taste (inasmuch as it reflects anything but the modern taste of Evans and his team of artists and architects). Only a few clay tablets have been found at Mycenae itself, but it is usually assumed that their paucity is a mere accident of preservation – the rest must have melted in rain instead of baking in fire.

The scribes of the Mycenaean palaces were important cogs in a complex, far-reaching and centralised administrative system, in which every sheep and pot of honey was counted for the purposes of taxation and distribution. This was a highly stratified feudal society with a *wanax* or king at the top, below whom spread a pyramid of lesser nobles, military chiefs and leaders of craft guilds, some of whom share the title *basileus* (a word that appears in the Homeric epics in a more exalted guise, also meaning 'king'). Lists of male occupations turn up a few surprising omissions, farmers, merchants and scribes being the most noticeable. The rather sketchy presence of women in the tablets also attests to the partiality of the record; they appear only as priestesses or menials, but the list of jobs of this latter group is evocative of Mycenaean daily life: corn-grinders, bath-attendants, flax-workers, spinners. Also mouth-wateringly suggestive is the following list: cardamom, celery-seed, coriander, cress, cumin, fennel, galangal, ginger, mint, pennyroyal, safflower, saffron, sage, sesame. Perhaps it is safe to say that Greek cuisine has not become noticeably more adventurous in the last 3500 years.

Entangled with the administration of the economy, and recorded in the same dry, bureaucratic tones in the tablets, are the offerings made to various deities, a sort of theological taxation in which great quantities of wine, honey, perfumed oil, wool, grain, fleeces, cloth, sheep, pigs, oxen and goats were dedicated to the gods. The names of the deities tended to confirm the long-standing theory of two predominant strains of Mycenaean religion in which the nature goddesses adopted from Crete coexisted with the Olympian deities brought along from the north. The Olympians whose names appear in Linear B are Zeus, Hera, Artemis, Athena, Poseidon, Ares, Hermes and, to everyone's surprise, Dionysus, usually thought to be a latecomer to the pantheon. Zeus and Poseidon both have female counterparts in the Linear B tablets, neither of whom made it through the Dark Ages. The goddesses of Cretan origin are honoured with their title *Potnia*, a word that survived as a form of respectful address in Homer meaning 'lady' or 'mistress'. There are various ladies in the tablets, the most romantic being the 'Lady of the Labyrinth' who makes a single but much-discussed appearance on a tablet from Knossos.

After Ventris' death, Chadwick's work on the Linear B texts attested to the fact that the narrative impulse dies hard even when the most rigorous philologist confronts the most fragmentary evidence. From the Pylos tablets, which had been baked hard in the fire that destroyed the Palace, Chadwick managed to reconstruct the poignant story of Mycenaean scribes recording the massing of the king's navy as word of an imminent invasion reached the unwalled kingdom. The argument is pretty elaborate and Chadwick finally has to admit that 'what actually happened remains a tantalising mystery'. Ultimately the picture that he is trying to paint emerges much more clearly from the archaeological evidence than from the Linear B decipherment: 'All we know is that the palace was looted and burnt. The absence of human remains suggests that no resistance took place there …'.

Meanwhile Mycenae itself was undergoing a post-war restoration. Between 1950 and 1957 the Greek Government Service for the Preservation and Restoration of Ancient Monuments, or Anastylosis, undertook a programme of reconstruction work at the site. Wooden scaffolding was erected in sections along the length of the wall and blocks that had fallen to the ground were identified and lifted back into place, including the replacement of two huge stones immediately to the right of the Lion Gate relief. The Anastylosis also rebuilt a corner of the main chamber of the Palace and restored the other entrance to the acropolis, the 'Postern Gate', a smaller, simpler version of the Lion Gate, now sporting wooden doors. Alan Wace's daughter Elizabeth witnessed the labour and later remarked that 'When we watched the work of the Anastylosis repairing the walls in the 1950s we came to realise that hard labour was more important than elaborate equipment.' The slaves who built the walls of Mycenae had become visible; those massive stones were not raised by giants, but by the Cyclopean political power that was required to marshal sufficient man-sweat to cut and stack thousands upon thousands of 2-tonne blocks.

In the spring of 1951 the Anastylosis undertook to repair one of the tholos tombs outside the acropolis, the so-called 'Tomb of Clytemnestra', which had been cracked open like a soft-boiled egg at some point in its history and emptied of its contents. As the workmen dug some clay with which to repair the top of the dome, a broken tombstone came to light, some of its fragments still standing in the base that supported it. The area underneath the tombstone was excavated, revealing a shaft grave similar to the ones found by Schliemann in the Grave Circle within the citadel. In November Dr Ioannis Papadimitriou, who was overseeing work in the Argolid, and Professor George Mylonas of Washington University, Missouri, came to inspect the site. They noticed three stones jutting out from the surface of the soil, just to the south of the newly opened grave, which seemed to belong to a curving wall. The following January a preliminary investigation revealed that a low rubble wall had, indeed, once delineated a circular enclosure almost as big as the one around the circle of graves in the citadel. Schliemann's Grave Circle now had an older sibling.

Grave Circle B, as this new discovery became known (while Schliemann's was renamed Grave Circle A), was greeted with great excitement. Here at last was a god-sent opportunity for modern archaeological methods to be applied to Mycenaean shaft-grave burials. Schliemann's descriptions of the shaft graves from Grave Circle A were vague and confusing, hampered by the fact that he had no idea what he was looking at and distorted by his determination to have found Agamemnon's tomb. Now came the chance to do the job properly. Over a period of two years the area within the new Grave Circle was cleared, exposing a total of twenty-four tombs, of which fourteen were shaft graves. The details of their construction, their relative dates, the positioning of the bodies and the arrangement of the grave goods were all meticulously worked out and recorded. The bones were measured and the stomach contents analysed. A physical anthropologist attempted a forensic reconstruction of the cause of death, concluding that some of the men, unusually tall for their time, had died in combat. More recently, even the faces of some of the dead were reconstructed from the skulls.

It seemed that Grave Circle B was in use for just over a century, between about 1675 and 1550 BC, overlapping with its younger, grander sibling for about sixty years. Although the finds were not as rich as those from the citadel, the shaft graves clearly contained royalty, interred in all their finery, with gold trimmings around the hems of some of their garments, or gold bands binding their wrists and foreheads, the females decked out with diadems, earrings, necklaces and gold-foil rosettes. Around the bodies their belongings and grave furnishings were carefully arranged: vases full of wine and oil and honey, bronze swords and daggers, vessels of silver and gold. One tomb contained what might be two portraits of the deceased: a death mask of electrum in exactly the same style as two of the gold masks found by Schliemann in the other Grave Circle, plus an amethyst sealstone with a jolly little bearded profile engraved on it.

During this period, Schliemann's Agamemnon underwent a temporary sex-change, metamorphosing from a bloodthirsty Aryan warlord to a homesick Egyptian princess. George Mylonas, one of the excavators of Grave Circle B, pondering the Egyptian influence on Mycenae, came to the conclusion that the well-preserved body that Schliemann had instantly recognised as the king of kings was, in fact, an Egyptian mummy. Mylonas acknowledged that this experiment with embalming did not catch on, as only one of a total of forty-three shaft-grave burials exhibited it, and proffered this romantic explanation for its singularity: 'It may even be suggested that the person whose body was embalmed was an Egyptian princess, who marrying and dying abroad, asked to be prepared for burial in accordance with the customs of her native land.' (To explain away the male death mask, he suggested that Schliemann must have either lied or been mistaken: 'Of course Schliemann stated that the mask was over the face of the embalmed body, but certainty on that score cannot be established.')

With the decipherment of Linear B completed and the finds from Grave Circle B published, the time was ripe for a major reassessment of all the evidence for the character of Mycenaean civilisation. In 1964 the American classicist Emily Vermeule published her *Greece in the Bronze Age*, a synthesis of the finds which, as a text for the general reader, has yet to be surpassed. In the introduction Vermeule said that she had altogether discarded the Homeric epics as evidence for life in the Bronze Age, remarking that it 'seems more honest, even refreshing, not to invoke Homer either as decoration or instruction'. In fact, the heroes are often invoked in her text, not as decoration or instruction, but as a useful source of evidence if handled with appropriate caution. Vermeule manages to honour the mythical traditions of the site without letting them overwhelm the physical evidence, and the result is a Mycenae in which kings and heroes convincingly coexist with potters and weavers.

Perhaps the most immediate puzzle for the present-day visitor to Mycenae is the contrast between the massive defensive walls of the site – the most prominent feature of the remains – and the peaceable characterisation of the Mycenaean Koinê in the museum. After giving a vivid summary of the defensive engineering of the walls of Mycenae and Tiryns, 'swung far outside the original palace plateau to protect outlying houses of commoners after 1250 BC', Vermeule confronts this riddle directly: 'these walls have always puzzled believers in a united mainland empire, for they are obviously at odds with any sense of political safety'. Her dark, but eminently plausible, conclusion is that 'the danger is certainly homebred and natural when polis [city-state] organisation is the rule.' Greek tradition has it that the various Mycenaean states were constantly attacking each other during the thirteenth century, and 'Mycenae itself was burned two or three times, surely by Mycenaeans'. As the later history of the Peloponnese demonstrates, constant aggression is not entirely at odds with great cultural achievements and a degree of cultural homogeneity, and Vermeule suggests that 'the general organisation of Mycenaean power had no more stability than a classical alliance among city-states'.

Another of the baffling questions raised by Mycenae is how it achieved its dominance over the Argolid when it was distinctly less well placed than Argos. Vermeule's integration of the legendary traditions of Mycenae into her overall understanding of the site allows her to speculate as to the role of human agency in Mycenaean history. Travelling back to the beginnings of Mycenae's glory, manifest in the 'furious splendour of the Shaft Graves', she asks the reader to imagine the gold-smothered princes as enjoying a life of 'raids, aristocratic battle training, and the amassing of portable loot ...':

> *The princes were few, no doubt closely knit by social or family ties which helped them impose their policies on a diffuse agrarian peasantry. They knew how to exploit local metals and metal technology. They had the training in new war techniques – the battle chariot and the long sword – to be pretty redoubtable in violent conflict. They had the intelligence to capitalise on trade*

with newly affluent Mediterranean regions. And they seem to have been fearless in foreign contact.

This is heroism as a political and material reality, neither revered nor reviled, but accepted as part of the fabric of ancient life.

When *Greece in the Bronze Age* was published, only one area inside the citadel remained unexcavated, a little stretch just south of the Grave Circle between a large villa first dug by Schliemann and a smaller house exposed by Tsountas. Throughout the 1960s a team from the British School led by Lord William Taylour worked with Mylonas and Papadimitriou from the Greek Archaeological Society to coax the last bit of the Mycenaean citadel into the light of day. The pace of the work amply demonstrated how much the modernisation of the archaeological enterprise had also involved its dramatic deceleration. It seems that archaeology is fractal in its geometry: the craft of excavation can be split into thinner and thinner layers, each of which can be subjected to more and more detailed analysis. This last bit of the citadel took seven seasons to dig, followed by over three decades of study. (Quite a contrast with Schliemann's four months at Mycenae followed by immediate publication.) The stratigraphy revealed almost the whole history of the site. Starting from the top Hellenistic layer, the archaeologists peeled away the detritus of nearly sixty centuries, down through Iron Age graves, through three different layers of Bronze Age remains, through graves of the prehistoric cemetery (the burial ground that included Grave Circle A), right down to traces of the earliest Neolithic inhabitants.

During the seasons of 1968 and 1969 Taylour and his

team finally reached the building layer contemporary with the Palace at the summit of the citadel. What they found there surprised everyone. Nothing remotely similar had ever been found before on the Greek mainland. Although altars and shrines had been identified, they were associated with palaces or private houses. Dedicated public places of worship were thought not to have existed in Mycenae. But here was a temple, a 'free standing building of cult purpose', still containing many of its idols and offerings. One terracotta statue was still in situ, standing on an altar just where it would have stood when the people of Mycenae came here to worship.

And what spectacularly ugly things some of the votive objects of Mycenae's 'Palatial period' turned out to be. The temple, a small square room entered through a vestibule, contained a low rectangular dais at its centre – possibly for receiving ritual libations – and a series of irregularly spaced narrow platforms of different heights against the far wall – presumably an altar. On the highest of these narrow platforms on the far right-hand side stood a large female clay idol, about 60 centimetres tall. She is the work of a potter, wheelmade, a hollow column of clay that tapers in and then flares out slightly before narrowing for the shoulders and neck and finally widening to denote the long oval head. Arms, breasts and facial features have been added to this central core. The arms, stuck into the cylindrical body of the figure like the handles of an amphora, are spindly and short. Only one survives complete, held aloft in front of the body. The breasts are small and jut out. The head is large and the face impressively hideous: a long hooked nose emerges from the top of the brow and overhangs the smirking mouth, the eyes bulge, the

[162]

23. The unbroken female idol from the Cult Centre at Mycenae, a bafflingly hideous votive object found in 1968 still standing on its altar.

ears are huge with pendulous lobes and the jaw is so heavy that it occupies nearly half of the head (illustration 23).

Next to the altar on which this fearsome creature stood, a flight of steps climbed to a tiny room, no more than a couple of metres square, in which dozens more of her fellows were found, all broken, but many of them susceptible to restoration. At some point the room had been walled off, indicating that the cache of idols was no longer in use. The figures are so schematic that it is not possible to determine with any certainty which are meant to be female and which male, but one analyst has suggested that the flat-chested idols with tresses are women and the barrel-chested, bald ones are men. These are objects that only their excavator could love. Taylour describes them as 'awesome' and 'forbidding', and remarks that 'each one has a striking individuality of its own'.

As we have seen, the Linear B tablets attested to the fact that the gods and goddesses of the male-dominated Homeric pantheon were already known and worshipped as early as the thirteenth century BC. Taylour suggested that the monstrous regiment of clay idols in the temple might represent these deities. Acknowledging that 'the idols, with their fearsome but very individual expressions are quite unlike the poetic descriptions of them in Homer', he then singles out one of the figures and drops a hint about who it might be: 'He is the tallest of them all and in his right, upraised hand he holds a hammer axe.' Even making allowances for the inadequacy of the plastic arts of the temple-potters of Mycenae, it is a little hard to accept that this statue represents Zeus. A mere 10 centimetres taller than the next largest figure, with staring eyes, and holding a little hammer next to his ear, the idol looks more like a DIY enthusiast who has just hit his thumb than the thunder-shaking father of all the gods. (These figures have since been reinterpreted as worshippers rather than deities.)

West of the temple was another well-preserved cult area, the so-called 'Room of the Fresco', dedicated to an aspect of the Mycenaean cult influenced – at least in style if not in content – by Minoan Crete. This long, narrow room contained a terracotta bathtub and three water jugs, possibly for use in a bathing ritual. The east end of the space featured an altar and a brightly coloured fresco portraying three female figures, two standing and one seated, who could almost have walked off the walls of the Cretan Palace of Knossos. One of them wears a typical Minoan costume, tightly cut and revealing a full, white bosom; the other two sport the rather less flattering, looser, off-the-shoulder fashions of the mainland. One of these ladies – the standing figure on the left – seems also to have adopted the more martial ways of the north, as she holds a sword or spear, and has been interpreted as a warrior goddess.

Since the late 1960s the egalitarian style of post-war archaeology has manifested itself in a shift away from the traditional approach of investigating high hills and promising mounds towards a more evenly distributed scrutiny of the landscape. Now a whole area is likely to be meticulously surveyed for evidence of human activity before any digging starts, a technique that has the effect of making more visible the lives of the people who lived and toiled in the shadow of their rulers' palaces and citadels. In the 1990s the Greek Archaeological Society and the British School collaborated on a survey of Mycenae that greatly extended their understanding and knowledge of the area outside the citadel walls.

An 80-acre settlement of some 6000 people seems to have occupied the terraced slopes below and around the citadel. In the fourteenth century BC, possibly at the same time as the citadel was first fortified, the town boundaries were definitively marked. On the maps produced by the survey team it appears as a diamond-shaped area with the triangle of the citadel tucked into one of the corners.

The long slope to the south was the ritzy end of town, boasting the grandest houses; to the north-west, the commercial sector occupied the Pezoulia ridge. One of the commercial buildings contained a series of storerooms for 500 new vases, arranged on shelves by shape and size, forerunners of the serried ranks of souvenirs for sale in the modern village. The main entrance to this building featured a stone loading ramp. Another, dubbed the House of the Oil Merchant, had a group of thirty jars from Crete, two of which still appear oily today! Four of the houses in the same area have been identified as government offices from the presence of Linear B tablets detailing the distribution of goods. One of these contained a group of sixty-nine small jars, possibly for the doling out of wine rations. Another building in the same group appears to have been used as a storeroom for imported pottery and a workshop for the assembly of inlaid furniture. The whole complex attests to the bureaucratic, centralised, complex nature of the Mycenaean economy.

Beyond the city and the immediate area, hundreds of excavations all over Europe and western Asia – often the result of 'rescue' archaeologists snatching the traces of antiquity from the jaws of bulldozers – have revealed the extent of Mycenaean trade. Roads wide enough for chariots and carts radiated out from the citadel, running along the contours of the landscape, linking Mycenae with the neighbouring cities. Setting out from the rocky coast of the Peloponnese, Mycenaean boats plied their trade across a great swathe of the ancient world from Egypt to Turkey and the Levant, and westwards to Sicily and Italy. The merchants exported wine, perfumed oil, olive oil and finely worked objects made of ivory, bronze and terracotta, and brought back tin, bronze and gold, elephant tusks, purple dye and spices. They established trading posts all along the routes that their sailors followed, some of which became small colonies.

The cumulative result of over a century of ever-more painstaking archaeological work is that the amount of available data for the Greek Bronze Age has become both overwhelmingly vast and dauntingly technical. Statements made by archaeologists have acquired much of the white-coated gravitas of the physical sciences, but this air of authority comes with a pervasive interpretative caution. The New Archaeology asks of its practitioners that they frame their questions (according to a rather idealised understanding of scientific method) as hypotheses that can in principle be falsified. It seems that there are very few grand generalisations about prehistoric Greece that can stand up to such rigorous inspection. Take, for example, carbon 14 dating. The introduction of this hard-scientific method for determining the age of organic materials from a dig has raised many more questions for Aegean archaeology than it has answered, stubbornly refusing to fit with more traditional kinds of chronological evidence. So the larger picture of the Aegean Bronze Age, although impressively rich in detail, is always forming and reforming, cracking along the fault lines of long-standing controversies or crumbling under the weight of analytical minutiae.

Since the mid 1980s a series of international conferences in Aegean prehistory has brought together archaeologists from all over the world to share their findings and hammer out their disputes. Each conference is organised around a broad theme such as mortuary practice, craft and technology, iconography, feasting or religion. The resulting volumes of papers, complete with transcripts of the discussions, are an invaluable resource for the student of the Greek Bronze Age, collating the latest evidence and analysis. They also attest to the state of the profession itself – now minutely specialised, vigorously democratic and affably argumentative, the archaeology of prehistoric Greece has clearly come a long way since it was the province of a wealthy few.

The theme of the 1998 conference was war and warfare. Introducing the proceedings, the archaeologist Jan Driessen suggested that 'the scars inflicted during WWII and its nuclear aftermath ... have largely mortgaged the discussion of military matters and made it an anathema in post-WWII archaeology'. In the published version of his talk, he cited a book by his colleague Lawrence Keeley, *War before Civilisation*, which documents this bias – the difficulties in obtaining funding for studies of prehistoric war, the widespread reinterpretation of fortifications as symbolic architectural gestures rather than defensive measures and the systematic denial of evidence for conflict. Indeed, at least one paper at the 1998 conference seemed to exemplify this trend: one of the giants of post-war Mycenaean archaeology, Spyros Iakovidis, gave a presentation arguing that the massive walls around the citadels of Mycenae and Tiryns were built as 'symbols of the exalted status and the power of their rulers rather than as fortresses' and that Mycenae's subterranean cistern may have been 'built for convenience rather than the anticipation of danger'.

It is hardly surprising that the Greeks should have embraced the 'pacific turn' in archaeology. The scars inflicted during the Second World War were a long time healing in Greece. Right on the heels of their 1944 liberation from the German occupation came a devastating civil war, followed by years of unstable and repressive governments culminating in the totalitarian military regime of 1967 to 1974. Seen in this light, the labels in the Museum of Mycenae characterising the Mycenaean Koinê as primarily cooperative and friendly (see p. 146) appear as an attempt to shift the emphasis away from those cycles of vengeance and self-destruction so often repeated in Greek history and so vividly emblematised in the myths of Agamemnon's city. Just as Aeschylus wrote a happy ending for the curse of the House of Atreus in the image of fifth-century BC Athenian reforms, so the Museum of Mycenae – an institution born of the democracy that was re-established in Greece in 1974 – projects a certain cautious political optimism on to the ruins of the Bronze Age. The results for Aegean archaeology of this shift in emphasis, it must be said, have been largely positive. Even in times of war life goes on, after all, and decades of meticulous work all across the Peloponnese have sifted out and analysed the neglected traces of ordinary Mycenaean existence, underlined and sought to explain the homogeneity of Mycenaean culture and honoured the great communal projects – the draining of the huge lake around the fortress at Gla, for example – that must have required cooperation between the palaces.

On the international stage, however, the winds of intellectual fashion have once again changed direction. After Spyros

Iakovidis gave his presentation to the 1998 Aegean archaeology conference on the purely symbolic nature of Mycenae's fortifications, a diverse group of other scholars stepped up to offer alternatives to his peaceable vision of the Bronze Age Greeks. Paper after paper sought to understand the Mycenaeans as the builders of a warrior civilisation, in which military prowess was both symbolically and actually the basis of wealth and status. Work on Mycenaean militarism appears to have picked up pace at the beginning of the 1990s, as though a post-Cold War rise in temperature engendered a more welcoming climate for the study of prehistoric warfare. Perhaps now that we no longer cower under the threat of mutually assured destruction, our need to pacify the past has become less urgent.

All the technical and analytical sophistication of contemporary Aegean archaeology was on show at the 1998 conference. Advances in the techniques of surface survey, interpretative insights into the Linear B texts and the application of theoretical models borrowed from sociology and anthropology were mobilised to argue for the belligerent character of Mycenaean civilisation. Much of this work emanated not from Mycenae but elsewhere, for example from Pylos in the western Peloponnese, site of Nestor's Palace. When it was first excavated, Carl Blegen puzzled over the lack of fortifications at the site. Did this absence indicate that Nestor's domain was 'a land of peace and quiet'? he asked incredulously. All this changed when a vast undertaking known as the Pylos Regional Archaeology Project arrived in 1990. Between 1991 and 1995 PRAP employed the most cutting-edge techniques of archaeological surface survey to examine 40 square kilometres of the area around Nestor's

Palace. Using electromagnetic equipment, the team detected subterranean changes in the soil that indicated some sort of submerged structure, 2 metres wide and 60 metres long, following the contours of the hill on which the palace stood. Known austerely as 'the anomaly', this ghostly artefact was interpreted as 'the remains of a massive fortification around the citadel'.

At the 1998 conference, one of the co-directors of PRAP used the discovery of the 'anomaly' to kick-start her discussion of Mycenaean violence. 'A historical sequence of destruction and construction at palatial centres', she asserted, 'is becoming increasingly clear as exploration continues.' Noting that 'these disasters have been attributed to earthquakes' she tartly remarked that 'the building of massive Cyclopean walls is not a useful response to an earthquake'. She concluded that the Mycenaeans 'built their fortifications because they perceived a threat from human enemies'. It seems that the fabled walls of Mycenae's citadel *were* built for defence after all. Two of her fellow directors at PRAP then developed the same theme, concluding that the scenes of military conquest on the walls of Nestor's Palace depicted actual instances of combat and formed the backdrop to large celebratory gatherings 'at which group identity was reinforced'. Not only did the king of Pylos and his soldiers engage in war, they also revelled in their victories. Perhaps most indicative of the shape of things to come, one of the more junior archaeologists presenting at the conference made her international debut with a paper succinctly arguing that warfare was *the* principal motor for the emergence of Mycenaean civilisation.

One of the most fascinating presentations to the conference discussed the relationship between military prowess and social status in Mycenaean Greece. This analytical tour de force distinguished among five successive periods of Mycenaean history. The paper began with the age of the first shaft-grave princes, whose success on the battlefield was an integral part of their claim to political leadership. It then suggested that once the social and political stratification of early Mycenaean society was completed, a period of uneasy peace prevailed between the different mainland centres, during which the military energies of the rulers were directed towards conquering the surrounding islands. This was followed by the epoch of the palaces, illuminated by the Linear B tablets, in which powerful monarchs ruled more by virtue of their divine powers than by their prowess on the battlefield. During the last phase of the Palatial period, however, the military ability of the Mycenaean elites came to assume more importance as the citadels suffered one catastrophic destruction after another. Unfortunately, neither the military prowess of the kings nor their supernatural powers could prevent the collapse of the palace civilization; the art of writing was lost and Greece devolved once again to small independent polities ruled by warlords. By emphasising changes over time and delineating two epochs during which the mainland polities might have been at peace with one another, this argument brilliantly integrated work on the Mycenaean Koinê into the overall picture of a warrior society.

Mycenae is unquestionably one of the wonders of the world. To walk under the Lion Gate or stand in the Treasury of Atreus is to make direct contact with one of Europe's earliest civilisations. It is to the science of archaeology that we turn to understand something of the nature of that civilisation – its strangeness as well as its familiarity, its incredible cultural and artistic achievements, its fiery end. As an archae-ological site, Mycenae ranks on a par with other Bronze Age palaces on the Peloponnese, but it is these ruins alone whose visibility through the ages and whose legendary fame connect us with the whole history of Greece. From Homer to Euripides, from the tragedians to Pausanias, from Pausanias to Seferis, the stones of Mycenae have endured and the name of the city has been spoken, uttered in that language that breath to breath stretches back 3500 years to the scribes of Linear B. It is the power of those stories that gives the site its significance far beyond the boundaries of Greece. As the legendary citadel of the king who waged one of the most famous military campaigns of all time, Agamemnon's proud acropolis stands as an emblem of one of the most enduring aspects of the human condition: our appetite for war.

The Iron Age Greeks worshipped the hero and propiti-ated the god of war in the ruins of Mycenae. The Athenian tragedians and historians who lived though the bloodi-est period of ancient Greek history revisited the story of Agamemnon to reflect upon their own civilisation's violent self-destruction. Centuries later, philhellenes and revolution-aries reclaimed the tombs of the heroes as the birthright of a modern Greek nation. After the shaft graves were exca-vated by Schliemann, Mycenae was hailed as the homeland of the ultimate warrior caste, an Aryan aristocracy to be emulated in pursuit of national and imperial victory. When those dreams of glory suffocated in the mud of the trenches, Agamemnon's Trojan campaign was recast as a Euripidean tragedy, a vision of inexorable calamity in which victors and vanquished suffered alike. In the aftermath of the ferociously mechanised Second World War and its nuclear dénouement,

the whole concept of military heroism – glorious *or* tragic
– was supplanted by an anti-heroic image of combat as brutal
bedlam, and Mycenae was pacified and democratised. Now
the Cold War is over and the warriors have thawed, stalk-
ing the ramparts of the citadel once again. Can we finally
acknowledge the battle-scarred heroes of Mycenae without
recruiting them to fight?

> Great suffering had desolated Greece.
> So many bodies thrown
> into the jaws of the sea, the jaws of the earth
> so many souls
> fed to the millstones like grain.
> And the rivers swelling, blood in their silt,
> all for a linen undulation, a filmy cloud,
> a butterfly's flicker, a wisp of swan's down,
> an empty tunic – all for a Helen.

> Seferis, 'Helen'

MAKING A VISIT?

The National Archaeological Museum in Athens has recently reopened after a long refurbishment, and is in splendid shape. The central hall displays the shaft-grave treasure, but before you plunge into the prehistoric rooms take a look at the sculpted slabs of stone that flank the entrance. These are the tombstones that Schliemann found standing in the middle of the Grave Circle above the shaft graves. Note how crude the carving is. They are incredibly ancient – approximately 1600 BC – and were preserved from the prehistoric cemetery and incorporated into the new Grave Circle when the citadel of Mycenae was rebuilt in 1250 BC. These, and the shaft-grave gold that you are about to see, are among the earliest surviving royal monuments in Europe. Schliemann knew a thing or two about securing his own immortality, but he was riding on the shoulders of giants. The illiterate rulers of Mycenae left a record of their passing for us to gawp at 3500 years later. So before you turn to the so-called 'Mask of Agamemnon', take a moment to remember that Mycenae is so immemorial that even the practice of mislabelling Mycenaean artefacts with Homeric names is older than most of the ruins in Greece.

When you finally examine that famous golden face, you will find that the ancient tradition of Homeric mislabelling is being upheld, though barely. The current label tells you that you are looking at a 'Gold death mask, known as the "Mask of Agamemnon"'. Remember that it was actually the mask that now hangs next to it – the big round one with the little crumpled mouth – that Schliemann decided belonged to the king, only because the face beneath it was uniquely well preserved and so he seized the opportunity to 'recognise' the features of the hero. The back of this case houses the three other masks that were found in the shaft graves (illustration 24). As you consider the five masks as a group, see what you make of the accusation – levelled, of course, by those implacable foes of Heinrich Schliemann, David Traill and William Calder III – that the Mask of Agamemnon is of late-nineteenth-century manufacture, commissioned by Schliemann from a goldsmith in Athens (see *Archaeology* 52 (4) for the debate).

The rest of the shaft-grave treasure surrounds the masks. Be sure not to miss the two gold baby shrouds that seemed at the time of their excavation to confirm Pausanias' testimony that Cassandra – the Trojan princess and prophetess who was brought to Mycenae as Agamemnon's concubine – was buried with her twin sons. (For my money, in the unlikely event that anything in these cases is found out to be modern, it will be parts of these – the fit with Pausanias is just too good.) Another object particularly exciting for Schliemann was the gold goblet with little doves on the handles, now in the case right in the middle of this room, which he decided corresponded with Homer's description of 'Nestor's cup'. Remember, though, that all this material has been dated to approximately 1600 BC; i.e. 400 years too early to have anything to do with the Homeric heroes. Overall, the iconography of the shaft-grave treasure – gold death masks and some

24. These are engravings of the gold death masks from the fourth shaft grave.
Schliemann exclaimed over these as 'individual portraits' of the dead heroes
whose faces they covered. In fact, they are representative of the two types
of highly stylised mask found in the shaft graves. The round one with the
strange smirk is similar the moon-faced mask that Schliemann found on his
'Agamemnon'. The one with the beetling brows is just like another from the
same grave and a further one made of electrum found in Grave Circle B.
The question remains as to how the unique handsome bearded mask fits into
the tradition.

of the more militaristic imagery aside – is overwhelmingly Minoan, betraying the influence of Mycenae's sophisticated southern neighbour.

The back of this room houses the objects from Grave Circle B, another sacred royal enclosure from an earlier cemetery. Grave Circle B was not lovingly incorporated into the fabric of the expanded citadel as was Grave Circle A, and was discovered only by accident in 1952. The objects are not as dazzling as the treasure from the later graves, but spare them a look, as the difference testifies to the precipitous rise in wealth and power that Mycenae enjoyed starting in the sixteenth century BC.

The next room houses material pertaining to the fabric of the great Bronze Age palaces at Mycenae, Tiryns and Pylos. To the left is a 3D model labelled, slightly misleadingly, 'The Acropolis at Mycenae and the surrounding area in the 13th century BC'. What this model actually depicts are the ruins of Mycenae as they stand today, with certain features such as the Grave Circle restored to their thirteenth-century wholeness. The same model is to be found at the Museum of Mycenae, but it is helpful to have a look at the whole site from above, as it were, before visiting the ruins.

In the right-hand corner of this room is a case filled with tablets from the palace at Pylos incised with the Mycenaean script, Linear B. On the same side of the room are the frescoes from Tiryns, which strongly betray the influence of Minoan Crete. On no account overlook the 'ivory triad', a tiny, exquisite sculpture of two women and a toddler that the archaeologist Alan Wace found in the acropolis of Mycenae and thought must have adorned a ceremonial sceptre. It is displayed in the right-hand of the three cases that occupy the centre of this space and is wonderfully eloquent (to those receptive) of the goddess-centred Minoan strain in Mycenaean religion. Behind the ivory triad is the 'Warrior Vase', with its appealingly cartoonish painting of soldiers marching, which has been interpreted as an image of Agamemnon's troops going off to the Trojan War (unlike the shaft-grave treasure, the Warrior Vase may actually be close to the right date).

The last room displays objects from the tombs and graves of Mycenaean Greece. The back wall of the space features reconstructions of the half-columns that flanked the entrance to the Treasury of Atreus, made of plaster with bits of the originals floating in it. (Much larger bits are to be found in the plaster reconstructions of the pillars in the British Museum.) Take a good look at these, as they work against the impression of Mycenaean beehive tombs as brilliantly engineered but rather crude and bare. These columns are a reminder of the elaborately carved polychrome surfaces that would have adorned the monuments. The central case in this room also sheds light on the lost contents of the Treasury of Atreus, containing as it does the few artefacts that have been recovered from unplundered beehive tombs.

SCHLIEMANN IN ATHENS

Schliemann's house, beautifully restored, can easily be seen, as it is currently occupied by the Numismatic Museum of Athens, at 12 Eleftherios Venizelou Avenue (this used to be called Panepistimiou Street and is often still listed as such in guide books), just a couple of blocks down from the University. His tomb can be admired at the First Cemetery of Athens, just south of the Ardittos Hill: after you come in the main entrance, it is on the left, facing out from the front of a high ridge. The two combined are a marvellous testament to the power of Schliemann's personality and perfectly project the image of a nineteenth-century hero in the neo-Homeric mould.

MYCENAE

The most useful item on sale in the ticket booth is an 'archaeological map and plan', consisting of an aerial drawing of what the citadel might have looked like in the thirteenth century BC, when the Lion Gate was built. It's not a beautiful thing, but it really helps make sense of the ruins. Remember to take a torch if (unlike Henry Miller) you can face the descent to the subterranean cistern.

The first priority has to be to visit the citadel itself, passing through the fabled Lion Gate (1250 BC – all dates should be regarded as very rough approximations). The heads of the lions on the relief would probably have turned outwards to face the visitor as there does not seem to be enough room for profiles. It seems likely that they were made of another kind of stone, possibly steatite, and attached to the rest of the sculpture by long metal bars, the holes for which can still be seen. Note also the large round holes in the lintel stone of the gate, where the bronze-clad hinges of the wooden doors would have turned. (The smaller Postern Gate to the north has been fitted with replica doors where the hinge mechanism can be seen in action.) To the left of the entrance as you come in is a little square niche in the thickness of the wall that Schliemann thought was a very uncomfortable guardhouse and is now thought to have been an altar.

To the right of the inside of the Lion Gate are the steps leading to the Grave Circle. Now the monument is all dug away, but it would, of course, have been filled in, and have had the tombstones that are on display in Athens standing in the middle. If you work your way round to the spot where the Grave Circle curves closest to the massive walls of the citadel itself and peer down into the deep space between them, you can see a stretch of the low circular wall that marked the royal enclosure in the original cemetery (1610–1490 BC). It was only when the citadel was rebuilt 250 years after the shaft graves had fallen into disuse, with the thick defensive walls built outwards to accommodate the sacred royal enclosure, that the level of the Grave Circle was brought up to its present height (1250 BC – the same date, in other words, as the Lion Gate). The height of the walls that were built to raise the monument attests to the reverence with which it was still regarded a quarter of a millennium after it was last used (illustration 25).

Leading up from the Lion Gate is the Great Ramp. Note that the stairs that begin the ascent are modern, as are the steps that lead from the top of the ramp to the remains of the palace. The palace is badly eroded and not much can be seen, but the layout of the ground-floor rooms, the outline of the great hearth and the bases of the four columns that surrounded it can still be discerned. Behind the palace the site descends through one of the grander neighbourhoods, featuring the 'House of the Columns'. Again nothing more than the layout can be seen but what remains is still evocative of a gracious colonnaded Mycenaean villa, with a fabulous view.

The great feature of the north of the site is the underground cistern (1210 BC). The steps are uneven and slippery

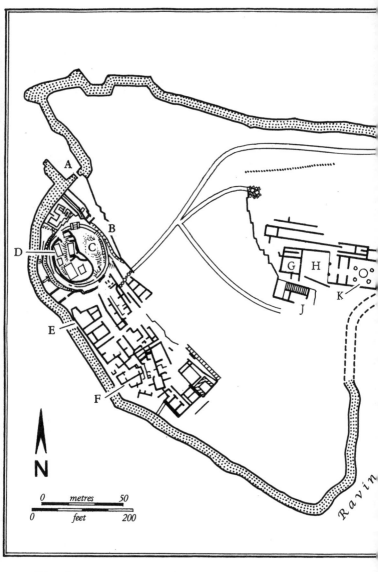

A

B

C

D

E

F

G

H

J

K

N

| 0 | metres | 50 |

| 0 | feet | 200 |

Ravin

25. Plan of the citadel of Mycenae showing the principal excavated structures.

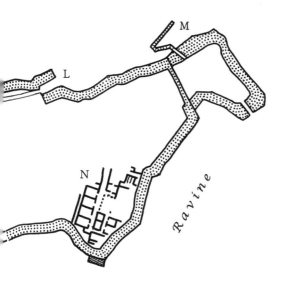

PLAN OF THE CITADEL OF MYCENAE

A Lion Gate
B Ramp
C Grave Circle A
D Shaft Grave where
   Mask of Agamemnon
   was found
E Warrior Vase House
F Cult Centre

G Throne Room
H Court
J Staircase
K Megaron
L Postern Gate
M Stair to Cistern
N House of Columns

and the darkness profound, but it is an experience not to be missed if possible. It ends with a rather baffling muddy floor, but this is just where the cistern has been filled in for the sake of safety. If Christos Tsountas was right, and it was designed to protect the water supply in the event of a siege, the sheer scale of the work that went into constructing it bears witness to the severity of the threat of war at Mycenae. From this part of the site, a path curves round past the Postern Gate, a smaller version of the Lion Gate. Just beyond the Postern Gate, some of the only ancient steps on the acropolis ascend to the lower terraces of the palace complex.

Outside the citadel, the main attraction is, of course, the Treasury of Atreus, but on the way have a look at the so-called 'Tomb of Clytemnestra', a slightly smaller beehive tomb just to the left of the path that runs from the Lion Gate. There are a few reasons for pausing here. This is the latest of the beehive tombs, dated to approximately 1300 BC, and so if any such person as Agamemnon existed, one or more of his direct ancestors may have been buried here. It is also one of the best places to appreciate the complexity of Mycenae's ruins. Right next to the tomb are the remains of the circular wall that surrounded Grave Circle B, Grave Circle A's older, humbler sibling, discovered in 1952 when the Tomb of Clytemnestra was being repaired. Unlike Grave Circle A, this royal enclosure was built over after it was no longer used, and the Tomb of Clytemnestra actually intrudes into it. The Tomb of Clytemnestra itself did not escape the same treatment. If you look on either side of the passageway that runs up to the entrance to the tomb you can see the remains of a curving row of stone seats from the theatre that was built here early in the third century BC, when Mycenae was taken over as a

26. The entrance to the Tomb of Clytemnestra. On the right you can see the curving row of seats of the Hellenistic theatre that was built over the tomb.

defensive outpost of nearby Argos. This one spot therefore contains what can be visualised as three overlapping circles, representing three phases of Mycenae's long history: Grave Circle B (1675 to 1550 BC), the Tomb of Clytemnestra (1300 BC) and the theatre of the Hellenistic Argive settlement (300 BC) (illustration 26).

On the north-west flank of the acropolis is the recently opened Museum of Mycenae. As a stand-alone introduction to the whole site, it is skewed towards the artefacts that have been most recently excavated, as all the rest ended up in Athens. Taken together with the National Archaeological Museum, however, it is a splendid achievement, very useful for evoking some of the daily life of the ordinary people of the Bronze Age. Pride of place is given to the figurines and frescoes from the Cult Centre, which amply demonstrate how very mysterious and alien the Mycenaeans remain to us. Don't neglect the room in the basement dedicated to Mycenae *after* the Bronze Age, which displays all the evidence for the cults of Agamemnon and Ares.

If you are staying more than one day in the vicinity of Mycenae, and are feeling energetic, you might want to climb the Prophet Elias, the taller of the two mountains that flank the ruins. The ascent starts with a fairly gentle road, but be warned that the last bit is really steep. In the late Bronze Age, Mycenae had a watch-post up at the summit, and the opening scene of Aeschylus' *Agamemnon* has a wonderful speech describing how the series of beacons announcing the fall of Troy communicated their message from one peak to the next until the light from the fires could finally be seen in the Argolid. Also, in the nearby village, check out the Belle Hélène pension, with the photos of the famous guestbook in the lobby.

FURTHER READING

CHAPTER I

Books on the history of Mycenae tend to divide into two categories – the literature narrating the exploits of travellers, antiquarians and archaeologists who went in search of the topography of Greek legend, and the volumes that explain the archaeology of the site. The story of the excavation of prehistoric Greece is well told in J. Lesley Fitton, *Discovery of the Greek Bronze Age* (London, 1995). An invaluable recent summary of the archaeology of Mycenae is to be found in Elizabeth French, *Mycenae: Agamemnon's capital, the site in its setting* (Stroud, Glos., 2002), from which my dates for the features of the site are taken. Michael Wood, *In Search of the Trojan War* (London, 1985) has a lot of material on Mycenae and is a beautifully presented account of the fascination with the Trojan conflict over the centuries. Still a wonderfully engaging introduction to the site of Mycenae is Christos Tsountas and J. Irving Mannat, *The Mycenaean Age: a study of the monuments and culture of pre-Homeric Greece* (London, 1897). Unsurpassed as a general introduction to the whole of Mycenaean culture is Emily Vermeule, *Greece in the Bronze Age* (Chicago, 1964). James Joyce's formula for historical truth occurs as Stephen Daedalus ponders the unfortunate career of King Pyrrhus in the first section of *Ulysses*. The quotes from George Grote are from volume I of his twelve-volume *History of Greece* (London, 1846).

CHAPTER 2

Good English translations of all the ancient Greek texts discussed in this chapter, including Pausanias' *Description of Greece*, are to be found in Penguin Classics editions, although I have used J. G. Frazer's translation of Pausanias (London, 1898). The impact of the Homeric epics in eighth-century BC and later Greece is brilliantly discussed in Anthony Snodgrass, *Archaic Greece, the Age of Experiment* (London and Melbourne, 1980). Hero cults are the subject of Carla Antonaccio, *An Archaeology of Ancestors: tomb cult and hero cult in early Greece* (Lanham, MD, 1995). Peter Hunt, *Slaves, Warfare and Ideology in the Greek Historians* (Cambridge, 1998) considers changes to the Greek way of waging war in the fifth century BC. The shrines and temples of later Mycenae are analysed in a series of articles in the *Annual of the British School at Athens* (*BSA*): J. M. Cook, 'The Agamemnoneion', *BSA* 48; Nancy L. Klein, 'Excavation of the Greek Temples at Mycenae', *BSA* 92; C. A. Boethius, 'Mycenae, the Hellenistic Period', *BSA* 25. Aeschylus' politically expedient rewriting of the Agamemnon story is thoroughly dissected in Anthony Podlecki, *The Political Background of Aeschylean Tragedy* (Ann Arbor, MI, 1966). R. M. Cook reconstructs what Thucydides would have been able to see of the ruins of Mycenae in his 'Thucydides as Archaeologist', *BSA* 50. For Euripides' rewriting of the Trojan War in the context of the Peloponnesian War see N. T. Croally, *Euripidean Polemic: the Trojan women and the function of tragedy* (Cambridge, 1994).

CHAPTER 3

An excellent survey of the history of travellers to Greece is Richard Stoneman, *Land of Lost Gods: the Search for Classical Greece* (Norman, OK, 1987). The exploits of the Dilettanti Society are the subject of Hugh Tregaskis, *Beyond the Grand Tour* (London, 1979). French travellers to the lands of legend are elegantly introduced in Olga Augustinos, *French Odysseys: Greece in French travel literature from the Renaissance to the Romantic era* (Baltimore and London, 1994). Lord and Lady Elgin's letters home from Mycenae are excerpted in A. H. Smith, 'Lord Elgin in the East', *Journal of Hellenic Studies* 36. The Marquis of Sligo's removal of the columns flanking the entrance to the Treasury of Atreus is narrated in F. N. Pryce, *Catalogue of the Sculpture in the Department of Greek and Roman Antiquities of the British Museum*, vol. I, pt 1, *Prehellenic and Early Greek* (London, 1928). Quotations from the Dilettanti and fellow travellers are from Edward Dodwell, *A Classical and Topographical Tour through Greece during the years 1801, 1805, and 1806* (London, 1819) and *Views and Descriptions of Cyclopian, or Pelasgic Remains in Greece and Italy* (London, 1834); Peter Laurent, *Recollections of a Classical Tour through Various Parts of Greece, Turkey and Italy, Made in the Years 1818 and 1819* (London, 1822); William G. Clark, *Peloponnesus: Notes of Study and Travel* (London, 1858); T. S. Hughes, *Travels in Greece and Albania* (London, 1830); R. F. Chateaubriand, *Itineraire de Paris à Jérusalem* (Paris, 1855); Abel Blouet, *L'Expedition scientifique de Morée*, vol. II (Paris, 1834), J. A. Buchon, *La Grèce continentale et la Morée: voyages, sejour et études historiques en 1840 et 1841* (Paris, 1843). Juliusz Słowacki's 'Journey to the Holy Land from Naples' is translated by Michael Mikos in *Juliusz Slowacki, this Fateful Power:*

sesquicentennial anthology 1809–1949 (Lublin, 1999).

CHAPTER 4

Schliemann is the subject of countless biographies. Leon Deuel, *Memoirs of Heinrich Schliemann: a documentary portrait drawn from his autobiographical writings, letters and excavation reports* (London, 1978), and David Traill, *Schliemann of Troy: treasure and deceit* (New York, 1995) are both highly recommended. Schliemann's own works provide blow-by-blow accounts of his excavations, and his *Mycenae: a narrative of researches and discoveries at Mycenae and Tiryns* (London, 1878) is a fascinating and wonderfully illustrated read (but see Traill for his frequent 'adjustments' of the record). His Mycenaean diary, which he kept in English, has been annotated and published in William Calder III and David Traill (eds), *Myth Scandal and History: the Heinrich Schliemann controversy and a first edition of the Mycenaean diary* (Detroit, 1986). David Traill's article 'Schliemann's Acquisition of the Helios Metope and his Psychopathic Tendencies' is in Traill and Calder (eds), *Excavating Schliemann* (Atlanta, GA, 1993). Still the most meticulous photographic record of the shaft-grave gold is Georg Karo, *Die Schachtgräber von Mykenai* (Munich, 1930–33). An excellent account of Frank Calvert's role in the excavation of Troy is in Susan Allen, *Finding the Walls of Troy: Frank Calvert and Heinrich Schliemann at Hisarlik* (Berkeley, CA, 1999).

CHAPTER 5

Gladstone's preface is in Heinrich Schliemann, *Mycenae: a*

narrative of researches and discoveries at Mycenae and Tiryns
(London, 1878). The politician's Homeric scholarship is discussed in Frank Turner, *The Greek Heritage in Victorian Britain*
(New Haven, CT, 1981). The quotation from Edith Durham
is cited in Mark Mazower, *The Balkans: a short history* (New
York, 2000). Aryan ideology is the subject of Leon Poliakov,
*The Aryan Myth: a history of racist and nationalist ideas in
Europe*, trans. Edmund Howard (New York, 1974). Malcolm
Quinn, *The Swastika: constructing the symbol* (London, 1994)
provided the leads to much of the material on the enthusiasm
for Schliemann's work among anti-Semites.

CHAPTER 6

Christos Tsountas and J. Irving Mannat, *The Mycenaean
Age: a study of the monuments and culture of pre-Homeric Greece*
(London, 1897) is the main source for the material in this
chapter. Karl Schuchhardt, *Schliemanns Ausgrabungen in Troja,
Tiryns, Mykenä, Orchomenos, Ithaka im Lichte der heutigen
Wissenschaft* (Leipzig, 1890) was translated by Eugenie Sellars
and appeared under the title *Schliemann's Excavations: an
archaeological and historical study* (London, 1891). The state of
Mycenaean archaeology at the end of the nineteenth century
is excellently summarised in the introduction to J. G. Frazer,
Pausanias's Description of Greece (London, 1898). The best biography of Arthur Evans is by his much younger half-sister Joan
Evans, *Time and Chance: the story of Arthur Evans and his forebears* (London, 1943). A meticulously researched but controversial recent life of Evans is J. A. MacGillivray, *Minotaur: the
archaeology of Minoan myth* (London, 1999). There is a potted
biography of Alan Wace in Rachel Hood, *Faces of Archaeology*

in Greece: caricatures by Piet de Jong (Oxford, 1998). Alan Wace, *Mycenae: an archaeological history and guide* (Princeton, NJ, 1949) comprises Wace's own account of his pre-war work at Mycenae and is also an excellent introduction to the site. Blegen's excavations at the Palace of Nestor are the subject of Carl Blegen and Marion Rawson, *A Guide to the Palace of Nestor* (Cincinnati, 1962). Again, J. Lesley Fitton, *Discovery of the Greek Bronze Age* (London, 1995) has a very helpful account of the archaeological developments between the end of Schliemann's excavations and the beginning of the Second World War.

<h3 style="text-align:center">CHAPTER 7</h3>

A good life of d'Annunzio is John Woodhouse, *Gabriele d'Annunzio: defiant archangel* (Oxford, 1998), from which is taken the excerpt from the poet's bloodthirsty 1915 speech. Jane Ellen Harrison's matriarchal interpretation of the Lion Gate is in her *Prolegomena to a Study of Greek Religion* (Princeton, NJ, 1903). An incisive analysis of Jane Harrison's life, work and reputation is Mary Beard, *The Invention of Jane Harrison* (Harvard, 2000). Hugo von Hofmannsthal's *Elektra* and its stunned reception in Edwardian London is the subject of one of the chapters in Simon Goldhill, *Who Needs Greek: contests in the cultural history of Hellenism* (Cambridge, 2002). The Homeric war report from the Gallipoli campaign is cited in Eileen Gregory, *H.D. and Hellenism: classic lines* (Cambridge, 1997). Oswald Spengler's prophetic historiography is analysed in Klaus Fischer, *History and Prophecy: Oswald Spengler and the Decline of the West* (New York, 1989). Malcolm Quinn, *The Swastika: constructing the symbol* (London, 1994) considers the deployment of Schliemann's work by the Nazis. H.D.'s letters from her time in analysis with Freud are collected in Susan Stanford Friedman (ed.), *Analyzing Freud: letters of H.D., Bryher, and their circle* (New York, 2002). The quotation from her war trilogy is from *Tribute to the Angels* (London, 1945). Freud's psycho-archaeology is the subject of many articles including Peter Ucko, 'Unprovenanced Material Culture and Freud's Collection of Antiquities' *Journal of Material Culture* 6 (3) (2001). The life and work of George Seferis are admirably chronicled in Roderick Beaton, *George Seferis: waiting for the angel* (New Haven, CT, and London, 2003). The finest English translation of Seferis' collected poems is by Edmund Keeley and Philip Sherrard (Princeton, NJ, 1995). The best source in English for modern Greek history is the work of Mark Mazower, especially, for the background to this chapter, *Inside Hitler's Greece: the experience of occupation* (New Haven, CT, 2001).

CHAPTER 8

John Chadwick, *The Decipherment of Linear B* (Cambridge, 1967 and many subsequent editions) is a gem. His *The Mycenaean World* (Cambridge, 1976) contains his reconstruction of the last days of Pylos. Grave Circle B (and the Egyptian princess theory for Schliemann's Agamemnon) are discussed by its excavator George Mylonas, *Mycenae and the Mycenaean Age* (Princeton, NJ, 1966), another clear and readable introduction to the archaeology and history of the site. Emily Vermeule, *Greece in the Bronze Age* (Chicago, 1964) cannot be recommended highly enough. The excavation of the Cult Centre is discussed in Lord William Taylour, *The Mycenaeans* (London, 1983). Oliver Dickinson, *The Aegean Bronze Age* (Cambridge, 1994) attests to the difficulty of extracting much certainty from the disputatious state of recent Aegean archae-ology. The papers from the 1998 conference on warfare are collected in Robert Laffineur (ed.), *Polemos: le contexte guer-rier en Egée à l'âge du Bronze* (2 vols., Liège, 1999). The indi-vidual papers cited (in the order in which they are discussed in the text) are: Jan Driessen, 'The Archaeology of Aegean Warfare'; Spyros Iakovidis, 'Late Helladic Fortifications'; Cynthia Shelmerdine, 'Pylian Polemics: the latest evidence on military matters'; Jack Davis and John Bennet, 'Making Mycenaeans: warfare, territorial expansion, and representa-tions of the other in the Pylian kingdom'; Phoebe Acheson, 'The Role of Force in the Development of Early Mycenaean Polities'; and Sigrid Deger-Jalkotzy, 'Military Prowess and Social Status in Mycenaean Greece'. The work of the Pylos Regional Archaeological Project can be viewed online at http://river.blg.uc.edu/prap/PRAP.html, and is also sum-marised in Jack Davis (ed.), *Sandy Pylos: an archaeological history from Nestor to Navarino* (Austin, TX, 1998). Lawrence Keeley, *War Before Civilisation* (Oxford and New York, 1996) discusses the pacific turn in post-war archaeology. A lucid account of the archaeology of the Mycenaean citadel is in Spyros Iakovidis, *Late Helladic Citadels on Mainland Greece* (Leiden, 1983), a highly recommended text that displays the virtues of the pacific turn at Mycenae. Again, one of the best places to go for the latest archaeological consensus about Mycenae is Elizabeth French, *Mycenae: Agamemnon's capital, the site in its setting* (Stroud, Glos., 2002). The extract from 'Helen' is from *George Seferis: Collected Poems*, translated by Edmund Keeley and Philip Sherrard (© 1967 Princeton University Press / Princeton, NJ, 1995); reprinted by permis-sion of Princeton University Press.

LIST OF ILLUSTRATIONS

While every effort has been made to contact copyright-
holders of illustrations, the author and publishers would be
grateful for information about any illustrations where they
have been unable to trace them, and would be glad to make
amendments in further editions.

ACKNOWLEDGEMENTS

I am very grateful to Peter Carson and Mary Beard for asking an untried author to contribute to such a distinguished series, and for their many editorial insights. The bulk of the text was written during a winter in Nauplion and I would like to thank the staff and librarians at the British School at Athens and Eutherpi Ralli of the Numismatic Museum of Athens for their assistance with the research. A special debt of gratitude is owed to an anonymous reviewer for Harvard University Press whose generous comments on the manuscript improved it beyond measure and saved me from many errors. On a more personal note, I would like to express my gratitude to my mother Charlotte Gere for the exquisite tact of her financial assistance during the writing of this book, and for the fine professional example she set as a veteran author. Finally, I thank my partner Hildie Kraus, not only for her sharp-eyed proof-reading, invaluable stylistic advice and cheerful encouragement at every stage of the writing, but also for the clarity of spirit, the sharpness of wit and the depth of understanding with which she makes everything possible.

INDEX

WONDERS OF THE WORLD

This is a small series of books, under the general editorship of Mary Beard, that will focus on some of the world's most famous sites or monuments.

Already available

Mary Beard: *The Parthenon*
Robert Irwin: *The Alhambra*
Richard Jenkyns: *Westminster Abbey*
Simon Goldhill: *The Temple of Jerusalem*
Keith Hopkins and Mary Beard: *The Colosseum*